MW01121466

Restoration Drama

Sean Elliott

GREENWICH EXCHANGE
LONDON

HUMBER LIBRARIES LAKESHORE CAMPUS
3199 Lakeshore Blvd West
TORONTO, ON.   M8V 1K8

Greenwich Exchange, London

Restoration Drama
©Sean Elliott 2013

First published in Great Britain in 2013
All rights reserved

This book is sold subject to the conditions that it shall not,
by way of trade or otherwise, be lent, resold, hired out or
otherwise circulated without the publisher's prior consent
in any form of binding or cover other than that in which it is
published and without a similar condition including this
condition being imposed on the subsequent purchaser.

Printed and bound by **imprint**digital.net
Typesetting and layout by Jude Keen Ltd., London
Tel: 020 8355 4541

Cover design by December Publications, Belfast
Tel: 028 90286559

Greenwich Exchange Website: www.greenex.co.uk

Cataloguing in Publication Data is available
from the British Library.

ISBN: 978-1-906075-79-8

In memory of
Michael Gearin-Tosh

Contents

Chronology

1642	Beginning of the Civil War
1649	Execution of Charles I; the Commonwealth rule
1653	Oliver Cromwell becomes Lord Protector
1658	Death of Cromwell, succeeded by his son Richard
1659	Resignation of Richard Cromwell
1660	(May) Restoration of Charles II; (June) the London theatres reopen; two patented theatre companies established: the King's Company and the Duke's Company
1665	Plague closes theatres.
1666	(2-5 September) Fire of London; (29 November) theatres reopen
1668	Dryden becomes Poet Laureate; Etherege, *She would if she could*
1670	Dryden, *The Conquest of Granada*; Behn, *The Forc'd Marriage*
1671	Buckingham, *The Rehearsal*; Wycherley, *Love in a Wood*; Behn, *The Amorous Prince*
1672	Wycherley, *The Gentleman Dancing-Master*
1673	Dryden, *Marriage à la Mode*
1675	Elizabeth Barry begins to act; Shadwell, *The Libertine*; Wycherley, *The Country Wife*
1676	Etherege, *The Man of Mode*; Otway, *Don Carlos*; Behn, *The Town Fop*; Shadwell, *The Virtuoso*; Wycherley, *The Plain Dealer*
1677	Dryden, *All for Love*; Lee, *The Rival Queens*; Behn, *The Rover*
1678	Dryden and Lee, *Oedipus*; Otway, *Friendship in Fashion*
1678-81	Titus Oates and the 'Popish plot'
1680	Lee, *Lucius Junius Brutus*; Otway, *The Soldier's Fortune*

1681	Lee, *The Princess of Cleves*; Behn, *The Rover, Part Two*
1682	Otway, *Venice Preserved*
1685	Death of Charles II, accession of James II
1686	Behn, *The Lucky Chance*
1687	Behn, *The Emperor of the Moon*
1688	The 'Glorious Revolution'; James II goes into exile
1689	Accession of William and Mary; Shadwell appointed Poet Laureate; Behn, *The Widow Ranter*
1690	Dryden, *Amphitryon*; Southerne, *Sir Antony Love*
1691	Southerne, *The Wives' Excuse*
1693	Congreve, *The Old Bachelor*
1694	Southerne, *The Fatal Marriage*; Congreve, *The Double Dealer*
1695	Southerne, *Oroonoko*; Congreve, *Love for Love*
1696	Cibber, *Love's Last Shift*; Vanbrugh, *The Relapse*
1697	Vanbrugh, *The Provoked Wife*; Congreve, *The Mourning Bride*
1698	Jeremy Collier publishes *A Short View of the Immorality and Prophaneness of the English Stage*
1699	Farquhar, *The Constant Couple*
1700	Death of Dryden; Congreve, *The Way of the World*
1705	Vanbrugh, *The Confederacy*; Centlivre, *The Basset Table*
1706	Farquhar, *The Recruiting Officer*
1707	Farquhar, *The Beaux' Stratagem*; Congreve, *Semele*
1709	Centlivre, *The Busy Body*
1718	Centlivre, *A Bold Stroke for a Wife*
1728	Cibber, *The Provoked Husband*

1

Beginnings

The Restoration of King Charles II in May 1660 came in a time of intrigue, religious tension and uneasy compromises. The Civil War, which began in 1642, embittered long-standing divisions in society. The victory of Parliament in 1648, the execution of King Charles I in January 1649 and in 1653 the replacement of the republican Commonwealth with the Protectorate of Oliver Cromwell, a military dictatorship, did little to heal those divisions. When Cromwell died in 1658, to be succeeded by his son Richard, order quickly broke down. Contending generals led their armies on London, but none managed to gain public support or to repair a rapidly collapsing economy, and it soon became clear that the least divisive remedy would be the restoration of the Stuart monarchy under Charles I's son.

Charles II was more interested in enjoying life than settling political scores, but his reign, whose chief purpose was to reunite the country, soon witnessed the execution of a few of those responsible for his father's death. These republicans were hanged, drawn and quartered, a public punishment which included hanging the victims for a time, disembowelling them alive, then dismembering them and displaying the heads on pikes. It was an intentionally public performance designed to warn malcontents of the fate awaiting any new rebels against royal authority.

There was another, less gruesome entertainment on offer from June 1660, when the London theatres opened again. Long censured by Puritans for their supposed incitement to licentious living, they were closed at the start of the Civil War amid fears of a plague and then kept closed by successive governments on moral grounds. Consequently Restoration theatre was born against a background of social, religious and political turmoil.

Charles ensured that the theatres remained under his control. He patented only two London companies, the King's Company and the Duke's Company, and the plays written during his reign were partly defined by his personality. Lord Halifax, in 'A Character of King Charles II', written soon after the King's death in 1685, describes this personality. Charles had an eye for human weakness: 'Where men had chinks he would see through them as soon as any man about him.' He distrusted everybody: 'He lived with his ministers as he did with his mistresses; he used them, but he was not in love with them.' Halifax puts the ministers and the mistresses together; like many Restoration comedy heroes, the King could be cold-blooded about both sex and politics.

Charles was famous for his wit. He kept heavy-drinking company, including George Villiers, the Duke of Buckingham, who wrote *The Rehearsal* (1671), a play about the theatre. Halifax disapproved, remarking that 'The wit of a gentleman and that of a crowned head ought to be different things.' The aristocracy, the Church and marriage were mocked; if they were attacked, how could the monarchy be safe? An anarchic wit runs through Restoration drama despite its royalist character.

At the beginning of the Restoration period the greatest changes in the theatre concerned every facet of performance except the plays themselves. The new theatres were not open-air buildings like the Globe, where many of Shakespeare's plays had been staged, and performances moved from the early afternoon to start around five in the evening. The theatres were lit by candlelight. They had a proscenium arch and a thrust stage, allowing for both tableau effects and for actors to come forward to address the audience. During the theatrical season, running from October to June, the revivals of old plays outnumbered the production of new plays by about four to one. Even a hit play could hardly run for more than ten days before the small number of regular theatregoers had seen it. With these continual revivals and adaptations of older pieces and translations of Spanish and French plays (especially Molière's comedies), the audience gained an impressive theatrical education.

A distinctive intimacy grew between the cast and the audience. Since the Restoration theatre followed the French example by introducing women actors (female roles in England had previously been performed by boys), this intimacy had a sexual element. The King took the actress Nell Gwyn as a mistress. Visitors would readily mix with the cast. The epilogue to Thomas Shadwell's *The Libertine* (1675) suggests that actresses might make themselves sexually available or the company could supply a friendly sixteen-year-old:

Some of our women shall be kind to you,
And promise free ingress and egress too.
But if the faces which we have won't do,
We will find out some of sixteen for you.

The new theatres housed about five hundred people. This audience was composed of the aristocracy, gentry and prosperous businessmen, and, mingling with them, prostitutes looking for customers. Since the theatre was considered disreputable both prostitutes and respectable women often wore masks ('vizards') to avoid being identified. The auditorium was lit throughout the performance, offering spectators a chance to look at each other as well as at the actors. Unsurprisingly, Restoration comedy, like its audience, often concentrates on fashion, appearance and disguise.

The beginning of Restoration drama can be placed in 1660 but there can be no definite date assigned for its ending. For some critics, that end came in 1685 with the deaths of Charles II and Thomas Otway, who wrote several of the finest Restoration tragedies. George Etherege and William Wycherley had stopped writing by 1680. Aphra Behn died in 1689, shortly after Charles' brother, James II, was deposed but the 1690s saw the rise of a second generation of dramatists who imitated their predecessors.

Restoration drama did not come to an abrupt close; it gradually changed with the changing character of the audience. In 1660 the theatre was primarily an entertainment for king and court; by 1700 the audience was largely composed of a new and prosperous middle class. The taunting of 'citizens' (City merchants) by Restoration playwrights has a defiant tone. Edward Ravenscroft's popular *The London Cuckolds* (1681) was one of many plays in which 'citizens' are cuckolded by their young wives and upper-class lovers. But the citizens steadily gained influence, and their business-orientated values of hard work and sobriety (not often the qualities of Restoration heroes) are increasingly reflected in the theatre of the early eighteenth century.

In 1698, Jeremy Collier's *A Short View of the Immorality and Prophaneness of the English Stage* called for morally responsible drama. It declares: 'The business of plays is to recommend virtue and discountenance vice.' Harassed by Collier's attack, William Congreve stopped writing plays after *The Way of the World* (1700). The death of John Dryden, the Restoration's major poet and an accomplished dramatist, in 1700 must have seemed symbolic. George Farquhar and

Susannah Centlivre carried the Restoration manner into the eighteenth century but tastes were changing. George Lillo's *The London Merchant* (1731), a tragedy set among the middle classes, concerns the seduction of an apprentice, George Barnwell, by a prostitute; their life of crime leads to murder and their executions. Lillo's play embodies Collier's wishes: crime is punished, sex unsanctified by marriage is condemned but honesty and hard work are rewarded. The emphasis is on deep feeling and sincerity instead of wit, and this reflects the rise of a 'sentimental' school of drama. The play gained international influence through the championship of Denis Diderot in France and G.E. Lessing in Germany.

Attempts to define the content of Restoration drama must be approximate. There are some frequently occurring elements, such as financial intrigue, a cynical view of religion, marriage and morals, and an emphasis on appearances. The plays often engage directly with the audience. Simon Callow, in *Acting in Restoration Comedy* (1991), discusses the use of the 'aside'. A character will say something which reveals his or her true feelings to the audience; this comment is 'unheard' by the other characters. Callow emphasises the meta-theatrical quality of the aside: 'It's a convention that very frankly says, "We're in a theatre."'

Callow claims that: 'The plays celebrate materialism and sexual licence.' He considers the attraction of this theatre for its original public: 'The plays were like living gossip sheets for a tiny metropolitan audience.' Harold Love suggests that Restoration literature's subjects resemble 'those of the modern daily newspaper – sex, politics, people, places, drink, sport, death, and a little religion'. Love's 'modern daily newspaper' and Callow's 'gossip sheets' evoke the informal chattiness of Restoration comedies such as Etherege's *The Man of Mode* (1676) but the comparison is harder to apply to a 'Spanish' comedy like Behn's *The Rover* (1677) with its depiction of political exile, or Dryden's *Amphitryon* (1690), which retells the myth of the hero whose wife is seduced by Jupiter.

Restoration drama is sometimes dismissed as possessing negligible literary value. The director Tyrone Guthrie, in *A Life in the Theatre* (1959), discusses the difficulty of getting educational funding to stage Restoration plays: 'Shakespeare, yes. Greek tragedy and the great classics of the French and German theatre, less definitely, but still yes. Restoration Comedy, very definitely no.' The situation has changed since Guthrie's time, but not enough. David Womersley's

Restoration Drama: An Anthology (2000) argues that the term 'Restoration drama' has for too long been 'synonymous with comedies written by men, set in London, focussed on sex and money, and sharing a common skeleton of plot'. Yet not all of the best Restoration plays are comedies, and an important contribution was made by women playwrights. The plays are not always set in London and can make significant use of their diverse locations. Other themes such as identity, political disorder and religion appear beside money and sex. This short book will support Womersley's argument that 'Restoration drama was innovative and even experimental, rather than passively formulaic.'

Restoration drama is more than insubstantial high-society comedy or exotic tragedy: it is a debate between novelty and tradition, freedom and law, atheism and faith, nobility and new money, all coloured by uneasy memories of the Republican era and urgent anxieties about England's future.

2

Sources

Restoration playwrights frequently rewrote material from other writers. Their approach to their sources resembles that of a modern screenwriter. Old plays could be adapted, as films are remade or inspire sequels. Wycherley's *The Country Wife* (1675) is a very free adaptation of a play by Molière. Behn's *The Rover* (1677) reworks Thomas Killigrew's *Tommaso* (1654) and Vanbrugh's *The Relapse* (1696) is a sequel to Colley Cibber's *Love's Last Shift* (1696). Ideas of originality, however, were changing in the seventeenth century. Shakespeare borrowed his plots freely but Dryden had to argue in his preface to *Don Sebastian* (1690) to defend an author's use of an existing story:

> Thus, of late years, Corneille writ an *Oedipus* after Sophocles; and I designed one after him, which I wrote with Mr Lee; yet neither the French poet stole from the Greek, nor we from the Frenchman. It is the contrivance, the new turn, and new characters, which alter the property, and make it ours. The *materia poetica* is as common to all writers as the *materia medica* to all physicians.

The Restoration playwrights are sometimes criticised for their treatment of Shakespeare's plays. But in their era Shakespeare did not possess his present cultural supremacy. In *Letters Concerning the English Nation* (1733), Voltaire asserts the long-established view that Shakespeare 'was natural and sublime, but had not so much as a single Spark of good Taste, or knew one Rule of the Drama'. Restoration authors saw Shakespeare as impressive but flawed. Dryden's *All for Love* (1677) refashions the sprawling material of *Antony and Cleopatra* into a disciplined text which obeys the three unities (events happen in one location, within twenty-four hours, and form part of a single 'action'). Otway wrote a version of *Romeo and Juliet* called *The History and Fall of Caius Marius* (1679), in which the heroine wakes after the hero has taken poison but before he dies, allowing the lovers to swear that they will meet in heaven. In 1681 Nahum Tate rewrote *King Lear* to let Cordelia survive and marry Edgar, while Lear goes into retirement. Elements of these versions continued to be performed into the nineteenth century.

Many characteristics typical of Restoration drama derive from pre-Civil War plays. John Fletcher's tragicomedies, often set in remote lands, influenced Behn and Dryden. Fletcher particularly among earlier seventeenth-century playwrights anticipates the bawdy humour of the Restoration. In *The Faithful Shepherdess* (1610) the sex-mad Cloe complains: 'It is impossible to ravish me,/I am so willing.' Philip Massinger is also an important influence. *The Renegado* (1624) resembles Behn's *The Rover* in its evocation of sex and danger in exotic locations. *A New Way to Pay Old Debts* (c.1625) anticipates the Restoration comedy of manners with its satire of business men. Frank Wellborn, impoverished through the duplicity of Sir Giles Overreach, asks a wealthy lady to treat him with exaggerated respect at dinner. This persuades Overreach and his followers that Wellborn is still a man of substance. They compete to do him favours. Wellborn exploits their expectations until he regains his wealth and marries Overrreach's daughter. Central to Massinger's play is the recognition that appearances are as important in business, where decisions are based on 'credit' more than on tangible wealth, as they are in fashionable society.

For many Restoration dramatists, England's greatest playwright was not Shakespeare but Ben Jonson. It is essential to recognise this in order to understand the kind of plays these authors set out to write. Thomas Shadwell declares in his dedication to *The Virtuoso* (1676) that Jonson is 'incomparably the best dramatic poet that ever was or, I believe, ever will be'. *Epicoene* (1610) was the first play performed on Charles II's return in June 1660. As R.V. Holdsworth says, 'For the Restoration dramatists – attracted, no doubt, by the play's concern with high-society manners and marriage, and its parade of wits, fops, and middle-aged grotesques – *Epicoene* was the great model for comedy.' Dryden regarded it as a perfectly plotted comedy and analyses it in 'An Essay on Dramatic Poesy' (1668).

Epicoene is set in London. Rural values are ignored or mocked, just as in the Restoration comedy of manners. Congreve's Millamant in *The Way of the World* (1700) declares: 'I loathe the country and everything related to it.' In *Epicoene*, Morose, an ageing bachelor decides to marry and to disinherit his nephew, Dauphine. Morose hates noise and wants a quiet wife. He is introduced to Epicoene and marries her. When the ceremony is over she begins to speak incessantly. The noise is increased by Dauphine and his friends Truewit and Clerimont, as well as some grotesque wedding guests. Distraught, Morose promises Dauphine never to remarry if his marriage can be dissolved. Dauphine pulls off Epicoene's wig and reveals that 'she' is a boy – so Morose is not married. The 'wedding' was Dauphine's plot to humble him. The revelation of Epicoene's gender is Jonson's meta-theatrical comment on the theatre of his time, when women's roles were performed by boys. It anticipates the frequent theatrical references in Restoration plays.

Epicoene also anticipates the predatory sexuality common in Restoration plays. Clerimont asserts, 'A man must beware of force,' but Truewit claims that women regard it as 'an acceptable violence'. Many Restoration dramas, including *The Rover* and Shadwell's *The Libertine,* evoke a society which tolerates this 'acceptable violence'.

Jonson was interested in the connection between appearances and speech. In his posthumously published *Timber; or, Discoveries* (1640), he suggests that deterioration of language indicates decay in a society: 'Wherever manners and fashions are corrupted, language is.' Good English is not found in academic discourse (Jonson and some Restoration Dramatists ridicule the specialist vocabularies of 'virtuosos'); instead, authors should strive 'in method and words to use (as ladies do in their attire) a diligent kind of negligence'.

Jonson's preference for clarity and a calculated appearance of ease (the oxymoronic 'diligent ... negligence') became the standard style of the Restoration. He declares: 'Language most shows a man: speak that I may see thee.' In this extract from Vanbrugh's *The Relapse* Lord Foppington speaks so that we may – all too plainly – see him:

> **Foppington:** I rise, Madam, about Ten a-Clock. I don't rise sooner because 'tis the worst thing in the World for the Complexion; nat that I pretend to be a Beau; but a man must endeavour to look wholesome, lest he make so nauseous a Figure in the Side-bax, the Ladies shou'd be compell'd to turn their Eyes upon the Play. So at Ten o'clock I say I rise. Naw if I find 'tis a good Day, I resalve to take a Turn in the Park, and see the fine Women; so huddle on my Cloaths, and get dress'd by One. If it be nasty Weather, I take a Turn in the Chocolate-hause; where, as you walk, Madam, you have the

prettiest Prospect in the World; you have Looking-glasses all around you – But I'm afraid I tire the Company.

Berinthia: Not at all. Pray go on.

Foppington: Why then, Ladies, from thence I go to Dinner at *Lacket's*, and there you are so nicely and delicat'ly serv'd, that stap my Vitals, they shall compose you a Dish, no bigger than a Saucer, shall come to fifty Shillings.

Between eating my Dinner, (and washing my Mauth, Ladies) I spend my time, till I go to the Play; where, till Nine a-Clack, I entertain my self with looking upon the Company; and usually dispose of one Hour more in leading them aut. So there's Twelve of the Four-and-Twenty pretty well over.

The other Twelve, Madam, are dispos'd of in Two Articles: In the first Four, I toast my self drunk, and t'other Eight I sleep my self sober again. Thus, Ladies, you see my Life is an eternal raund O of Delights.

Foppington's pleasures are based in the London his audience knew. His affected pronunciation ('bax' for box, 'raund' for 'round') embodies Jonson's point that decadent social values are revealed through corrupted speech. Foppington is a 'fop', a fool obsessed with the trivialities of cutting a fine figure among grand friends. Callow remarks that 'Fops are narcissists, not homosexuals.' Foppington is generous in his narcissism; he believes that women would rather see him than actors at a play; he loves the mirrors in the chocolate house because his multiplied reflection is, he assumes, a delight to everyone there. His claim that he 'huddles' on his clothes is ironic since it takes him three hours to dress, suggesting the extent of his self-adoration. He identifies price with value (his dinner is expensive so it must be good) and treats with religious solemnity what we call brand names – the more ostentatious and exclusive the better. In Etherege's *The Man of Mode*, Sir Fopling Flutter ecstatically lists these names:

Lady Townley: The suit?
Sir Fopling: Barroy.
Emilia: The garniture?
Sir Fopling: Le Gras.
Medley: The shoes?
Sir Fopling: Piccar.
Dorimant: The periwig?
Sir Fopling: Chedreux.

Lady Townley, Emilia: The gloves?
Sir Fopling: Orangerie. You know the smell, ladies.

Sir Fopling's recitation of the names is delivered with the reverence of a catechism. There are frequent jokes in Restoration plays about the fop's uselessness. Foppington claims his life is 'an eternal raund O of Delights'; the 'O' is a zero as well as a circle. A fop is a consumer who produces nothing but himself.

The fop comically exaggerates a concern with appearances which is pervasive among the Restoration aristocracy. Women wore clothes which accentuated their femininity, including low-cut bodices (as Callow says, 'Cleavage is a necessity'). Gentlemen valued elegance but they also wore swords. A gentleman would fight a duel to avenge any insult to his honour. Any hint of a wife's indiscretion or adultery could end in the death of husband or lover. Besides the fop, elegance of dress and manners is the mark of another archetypal character in Restoration drama: the libertine. The fop is harmless but the libertine could be murderous.

3

Libertines and 'Acceptable Violence'

The Puritans aimed to implement God's law in Britain. Adultery became a capital offence in 1650 (although this law was never enforced) because it is condemned in the Seventh Commandment. This partly accounts for the fixation on extramarital relationships in Restoration dramas. The Royalists argued that laws to enforce morality do not create better people but merely better hypocrites. In *The English Sappho* (1948; revised 1989), George Woodcock claims that brothels in London reached a record number under the Commonwealth. The Restoration dramatists generally associate extreme religious views with hypocrisy. In the late seventeenth century, according to Harold Love, the word 'libertine' was closer in meaning 'to the modern "anarchist" than "sensualist"'.

The claim that the libertines adopted a definite philosophy deserves some scepticism. A taste for promiscuity and heavy drinking is not restricted to deep thinkers. Etherege confessed that he was no great reader and merely wrote about his society but the archetypal libertine of the age, John Wilmot, Earl of Rochester, on whom Dorimant in *The Man of Mode* is based, was well read, an important poet and an emblematic figure in the Restoration theatre. Dryden dedicated *Marriage à la Mode* (1673) to Rochester and gave him a draft of the play to ensure the accuracy of the court dialogue. Elizabeth Barry, the leading actress of her time, is thought to have taken acting lessons from him. Samuel Johnson's 'Life of Rochester' (in *Lives of the English Poets*, 1779–81) states that the poet 'pursued low amours in mean disguises, and always acted with great exactness and dexterity the characters which he assumed'.

Libertinism was theoretically based on the moral teaching of the Greek philosopher Epicurus (341–270 BC) as transmitted by Lucretius (*c.*99–55 BC) in his Latin philosophical epic *De Rerum Natura* (*On the Nature of the Universe*). Thomas Creech's English translation of Lucretius was published in 1682 but well before then

English philosophical writers had begun to study and translate the poem. Epicureanism is a materialist/rationalist philosophy. Lucretius argues against the belief in life after death. He dislikes organised religion, denouncing priests as exploiters of their followers for personal gain. He does not believe that the gods intervene in our world. Only Venus, the goddess of love, has power over us and she is not an individual but an impersonal life force. In Book IV of the poem, Lucretius discusses love and sex. Epicureans deplore excess, including extremes of love. Paradoxically, Lucretius recommends promiscuity as an antidote to an overwhelming passion for one person. Dryden's translation of the passage captures the rakish tone of a Restoration libertine:

> But strive those pleasing fantomes to remove,
> And shun th'Aerial images of Love
> That feed the flame: When one molests thy mind
> Discharge thy loyns on all the leaky kind.

Heavy drinking was encouraged among mid-century Cavaliers. It became a sign of manly honesty in an era of political suspicion. John Oldham declares, in 'The Careless Good Fellow', 'He has no room for Treason, that's top-full of Wine.' (Women, on the other hand, were not meant to drink to excess; Mirabell insists in the marriage contract scene of *The Way of the World* that his bride may not keep certain alcoholic 'medicines'.)

The libertine is distinguished from other heavy drinkers or sexually voracious men by his nihilism. The heavy-drinking Sir Oliver Cockwood in Etherege's *She Would if She Could* (1668) is not a libertine. He visits London to pick up women and in the third act proposes a competitive orgy with three other men and a party of prostitutes. But he believes in God, the King and the social system which gives him his privileged position. He loves his equally unfaithful wife and when he comes to die he will do so as a Christian.

Libertines, by contrast, regard the values of their society as a fraud. In 'A Satyr against Reason and Mankind', Rochester attacks religious and political institutions as organised deceptions to keep certain individuals in power by oppressing everybody else; they use 'False freedoms, holy cheats, and formal lies / Over their fellow slaves to tyrannize'.

The libertine asserts the pointlessness of all human activity in his self-defeating pursuit of pleasure. His vices would ultimately subvert themselves. Prolonged heavy drinking impairs sexual performance and promiscuity made contracting the pox or clap (syphilis, gonorrhoea) almost inevitable. The long-term effects of syphilis were visible in the theatre. The first patentee of the Duke's Company, Sir William Davenant lost his nose to what Samuel Johnson calls 'mishaps among the women'.

Etherege and Shadwell offer contrasting dramatic treatments of libertines. The differences are partly due to the diverse backgrounds of the two playwrights. Etherege was an amateur dramatist and wrote only three plays. Like Congreve, who also produced a small body of work, he was a gentleman first and a playwright second. Shadwell, like Aphra Behn, was a professional and depended on his earnings. He wrote prolifically. Authors were paid every third night's takings from their plays, and if a production ran only for one or two nights the author earned nothing. Another source of revenue came from publishing a play with a flattering dedication to a wealthy patron. Etherege could address his audience as equals; to Shadwell they were his employers.

In *The Libertine* Shadwell offers moral condemnation of his anti-hero as well as criticism of a society which tolerates such adventurers. The play gives a repellent portrayal of unrestrained lust. The Don Juan story had already been treated by several European dramatists including Molière. Don Juan (Mozart's Don Giovanni) is a compulsive seducer finally confronted by the statue of a man he murdered while trying to force himself on his victim's daughter. The statue warns Don Juan to repent, but the hero mockingly invites this 'stone guest' to a midnight supper. The statue arrives at the appointed time and drags the seducer down to hell.

Shadwell's Don John declares, 'My business is my pleasure: that end I will always compass without scrupling the means.' His use of the word 'business' is apt, Don John follows a capitalist model of endless consumption. Shadwell gives his libertine two followers. These companions are not friends but competitors, acknowledging Don John's primacy. Women are his currency. He values quantity over quality, declaring, 'What an excellent thing is a woman before enjoyment and how insipid after it!' He is defined by the scale of his consumption; he is not interested in individuals and the play risks monotony in its lack of interest in individual psychology. Don John's two followers are indistinguishable from each other, his victims a complaining multitude. But Shadwell's focus is on the communities destroyed by the three Dons. Those societies are vulnerable through their flawed values. Don Francisco, for instance, benignly welcomes the Dons to his apparently harmonious and orderly home after they have been shipwrecked but his daughters are frustrated at the restrictive social roles imposed on women. Clara makes a standard Restoration comparison between the freedom enjoyed by English women and the restraint endured in Spain: 'There, they say, a lady may choose a footman and run away with him if she likes him, and no dishonour to the family.' Flavia adds that in England 'wives run and ramble whither and with whom they please'. Shadwell's audience would not have liked the idea of their daughters eloping with servants or their wives 'rambling' (looking for casual sexual encounters). Francisco's daughters sing about their situation:

> Woman who is by nature wild
> Dull bearded man encloses;
> Of nature's freedom we're beguiled
> By laws which man imposes.

The sisters share many of Don John's libertine views. He too thinks of nature in terms of unlimited desire: 'Virtue and honour! There's nothing good or ill but as it seems to each man's natural appetite.'

Shadwell calls his play a tragedy but Don John is without tragic dignity or self-awareness. Although the statue's intervention suggests God's justice, the moral intent is uncertain. At the beginning of Act III the three Dons escape from their shipwreck while better men drown. The ship's captain sees the storm in supernatural terms: 'These unheard-of prodigies amaze me.' But Don John is only aware of the 'farting and the belching of a cloud'. His concept of 'nature' does not include the natural world. He scarcely notices the tempest. His 'nature' is a free economy, allowing him to pursue his business without hindrance. His business ethic is seen clearly when he destroys a pastoral community of shepherds and nymphs. This community too lives by the laws of nature, but a nature very different from Don John's. As one of the shepherds explains,

> In humble cottages we have such content
> As uncorrupted nature does afford,
> Which the great, that surfeit under gilded roofs
> And wanton in down beds, can never know.

The three Dons attack the shepherds and rape the nymphs but Shadwell's sympathies are not with the victims. If the shepherds lived in an ideal community, they should have defended it properly. *The Libertine* depicts competing ideologies and suggests that, once God's dubious justice is removed, it is not the most civilised that survive but the most ruthless. *The Libertine* is not a tragedy – it is a business plan.

Libertinism is also an important theme in Shadwell's *The Virtuoso* (1676), although his primary satirical target here is scientific research and the recently founded Royal Society. Shadwell's satire scores some hits (Sir Nicholas Gimcrack swims on dry land because he is interested in the 'theoretical' aspects of swimming). The play begins with Bruce's outcry: 'Thou great Lucretius!' As Bruce puts it, Lucretius demonstrated that 'Poetry and good sense may go together.' He quotes six lines in Latin asserting that the gods neither reward the good nor punish sinners. Rochester loved these lines and translated them as an independent lyric:

> The gods, by right of nature, must possess
> An everlasting age of perfect peace;
> Far off removed from us and our affairs;
> Neither approached by dangers, or by cares;
> Rich in themselves, to whom we cannot add;
> Not pleased by good deeds, nor provoked by bad.

The subplot of *The Virtuoso* shows success coming not to the virtuous but to the cunning. Lady Gimcrack is a female libertine. She pays her lover Hazard for his services. Of 'keeping' (a regular lover) she argues: 'I know not why we ladies should not keep as well as men sometimes.' In the fifth act, during a masked ball, she pretends to be each of her two nieces in turn and has sex with their two lovers in rapid succession. Her husband finally realises the extent of her adulteries, but Shadwell does not punish her. She has an independent fortune and decides to live openly with Hazard.

By contrast, Etherege's three plays portray libertines sympathetically. Rochester in 'Timon' has a fool declare that Etherege had 'writ two talking plays without one plot' (the poem predates Etherege's *The Man of Mode*). With each succeeding play, Etherege laid greater emphasis on 'talking' rather than action. *The Comical Revenge, or Love in a Tub* (1664), set during the Commonwealth, contains one threatened and one actual duel, an assassination attempt and a persecuted Cavalier hero. *She Would if She Could* is a more conventional farce in which Sir Oliver Cockwood and his wife visit London, both on the lookout for lovers; they keep choosing the same places for their assignations and have to invent improbable excuses every time they meet. Finally, *The Man of Mode* (1676) consists of a series of conversations in largely domestic settings. There are no physical fights and no drunken parties.

Etherege's three plays have much in common. Frederick in *The Comical Revenge* is introduced in his nightgown nursing a hangover and he finally marries off his mistress to a foolish knight before his own marriage. Dorimant in *The Man of Mode* first appears in his nightgown wondering how to discard his mistress; he ultimately humiliates Mrs Loveit and becomes engaged to an heiress. Courtall too, in *She Would if She Could*, is first seen in the morning although he has dressed. Like Dorimant, he is soon visited by a procuress bringing news of a lady just arrived in London; he too marries an heiress.

Frederick, Courtall and Dorimant are elegant, socially adept and sadistic. Frederick takes pleasure in marrying off his discarded mistress, pretending that she is his wealthy sister, to Sir Nicholas Cully. Courtall pretends to love the ageing Lady Cockwood so that he can see the girl he really loves. Dorimant humiliates Mrs Loveit, remarking: 'Next to the coming to a good understanding with a new mistress, I love a quarrel with an old one.' The very names of Lady Cockwood and Mrs Loveit mock the obviousness of their desires (the one would like some cock and the other 'loves it'). By contrast, the women who marry the heroes maintain their poise.

Clothes are an important theme; all three plays contain an unsuitably dressed character. Dorimant shows himself a true man of his time when he declares: 'I love to be well dressed, sir, and think it no scandal to my understanding.' This standard is subverted in *The Comical Revenge* when Dufoy is drugged and locked into a sweating barrel used in treating syphilis. He becomes a walking symbol of the perils of a fashionable gentleman's promiscuity. In *She Would if She Could*, Sir Oliver's wife forces him to wear a 'penitential suit', designed to shame him into staying at home. When Sir Oliver goes to an inn to meet prostitutes even the hardened pimp, Rake-hell, is shocked by his client's appearance: 'Your black Cap and Border is never wore but by a Fiddler or a Waiter.' *The Man of Mode* introduces the absurdly overdressed Sir Fopling Flutter, who, according to Dorimant, 'went to Paris a plain, bashful English blockhead and is returned a fine, undertaking French fop'.

Sir Fopling asserts that Paris is his standard of excellence:

> Dorimant, let me embrace thee, without lying I have not met with
> any of my acquaintance, who retain so much of Paris as thou dost,
> the very air thou hadst when the marquise mistook thee i'th'
> Tuileries, and cried 'Hey chevalier', and then begged thy pardon.

Sir Fopling is over-friendly. He employs the informal second-person forms 'thee' and 'thou' (equivalent to the French *tu*), used for close friends, children and social inferiors. Dorimant icily responds by addressing Sir Fopling as 'Sir' and using the formal 'you'. Sir Fopling recalls a marquise who assumed that the impeccably dressed Dorimant must be a fellow French aristocrat (Sir Fopling would love to be the subject of the same mistake). His passion for France partly reflects the values of English Restoration society. The King's sister married into the French royal family. Wealthy Englishmen often finished their educations in France. Woodall, in Dryden's *The Kind Keeper* (1678), has just returned from a French academy. Restoration playwrights borrowed heavily from French comedy and the idea of the libertine had in part come to England from French writers such as Pierre Gassendi. Sir Fopling plays on English fears that London is a second-rate Paris but Etherege turns such anxieties to laughter.

Etherege's last comedy, *The Man of Mode*, is his masterpiece because it most closely resembles the 'talking' play without a plot described in Rochester's poem. There are actually two very slight plots. In the first, Dorimant frees himself from Mrs Loveit, has sex with Bellinda and becomes engaged to Harriet. The three women are Dorimant's past, present and future and, as a libertine, it is fitting that his life is seen in sexual terms. In the subplot, Bellair and Emilia defy their parents and marry. The portrayal of young lovers outwitting their elders is an old comic stand-by, derived from the Roman comedies of Plautus (*c.*254-184 BC).

With *The Man of Mode*, Etherege realises that his subject is society as theatre. His characters assume their parts as we watch. Dorimant and Mrs Loveit are seen at their dressing tables like actors preparing before going onstage. Sir Fopling Flutter travels to Paris to learn to play Sir Fopling Flutter. Mrs Loveit is the tormented heroine of her own tragedy and Harriet is dissatisfied with playing a country innocent. In their mock courtship performed to deceive their watching parents, Harriet and Bellair give each other directions like actors learning a scene:

Harriet: Smile and turn to me again very sparkish.

Bellair: Will you take your turn and be instructed?

Harriet: With all my heart.

Bellair: At one motion play your fan, look down upon it, and tell the sticks with a finger.

Harriet: Very modish.

Bellair: Clap your hand up to your bosom, hold down your gown, shrug, draw up your breasts, and let 'em fall. Again, gently, with a sigh or two.

Bellair's repeated references to Harriet's breasts suggest his rising excitement and create a joke about theatrical illusion: play-acting the attraction is making it real.

Dorimant is the greatest actor. On a literal level, he deceives Mrs Woodville with a false name to visit her daughter. Mrs Woodville has heard that Dorimant is a libertine and 'delights in nothing but in rapes and riots' – perhaps an ironic reference to Shadwell's Don John. Dorimant has no taste for violence. His feelings are cryptic. He teases Mrs Loveit with the libertine paradox that declarations of everlasting love only apply to that moment: 'To say truth, in love there is no security to be given for the future.' Even his love for Harriet is ambivalent. In an aside, he declares 'I love her, and dare not let her know it. I fear she has an ascendant o'er me and may revenge the wrongs I have done her sex.' By contrast, he tells Bellair: 'You wed a woman, I a good estate' – suggesting that his motives for marrying are financial, although this boast may be intended to disguise the depth of his love. Bonamy Dobrée in his *Restoration Comedy 1660–1720* (1924) says that Etherege 'presented life treated purely as appearance'; Dorimant is an immaculate surface with no awareness of its own depths.

The Man of Mode rapidly became a classic. It embodies the traits associated with the comedy of manners. It is set in London among the upper classes, the plot revolves around witty, suggestive conversations, there is the threat of the exposure of a scandal and an adroit manipulation of enemies. A fop and some rural characters are mocked, while the ending concerns several marriages of doubtful happiness. Restoration comedy extends beyond this limiting definition but Etherege perfected an influential model. Algernon in Oscar Wilde's *The Importance of Being Earnest* (1895) declares: 'If the lower orders don't set us a good example, what on earth is the use of them?' He echoes Dorimant's 'Whoring and swearing are vices too genteel for a shoemaker.' Both witticisms subvert the idea that the nobility rule through moral authority. Morality is hard work and so better left to the working classes.

Shadwell, Etherege and Wycherley depict libertinism in different ways. Shadwell emphasises the remorseless, methodical and business-like proceedings of the libertine. Etherege depicts the playful theatricality of seduction. Wycherley portrays the libertine's hunting ground: the unhappy marriage.

4

William Wycherley and the Dance of Cuckolds

William Wycherley wrote only four plays, but he is the most contro-versial of the Restoration playwrights. The harshest attack on him is Thomas Babington Macaulay's review of Leigh Hunt's *Comic Dramatists of the Restoration* (1841). Macaulay deplores Restoration comedy's depiction of adultery: 'All the agreeable qualities are always given to the gallant. All the contempt and aversion are the portion of the unfortunate husband.' Wycherley is the chief offender: 'Wycherley's indecency is protected against the critics as a skunk is protected against the hunters. It is safe because it is too filthy to handle.'

Macaulay opposes Charles Lamb's important defence of Restoration comedy in 'On the Artificial Comedy of the Last Century' (1822). Lamb had argued that Restoration comedies create a harmless fantasy of sexual liberty: 'the Utopia of gallantry, where pleasure is duty, and the manners perfect freedom.' While adultery should be condemned in the real world, Lamb argues, it is naïve to assess stage characters by the same standards: 'We substitute a real for a dramatic person, and judge him accordingly.' Critical debate about Restoration comedy frequently follows the fault line between Lamb's aesthetic approach and Macaulay's ethical one.

Wycherley's own audience saw him as a moralist. He became identified with Manly, the hero of his *The Plain Dealer* (1676), who exposes hypocrisy with a masculine frankness. Voltaire notes that while Wycherley borrowed his plots from Molière, he goes further than the French dramatist in his outspoken moral criticism. In his *Letters Concerning the English Nation* (1733), Voltaire distinguishes Wycherley for his forcefulness: 'Mr Congreve's Comedies are the most witty and regular, those of Sir John Vanbrugh most gay and humorous, and those of Mr Wycherley have the greatest force and spirit.'

In the 1920s, Bonamy Dobrée championed a reassessment of Wycherley's reputation. His work led to several important revivals of *The Country Wife* (1675). Dobrée's *Restoration Comedy 1660-1720* captures the cynicism of a generation that had seen its elders die during the First World War. Dobrée remarks appreciatively that Wycherley's 'satire almost reaches the level of fanaticism'. His work is 'tinged with a deep pessimism, a fierce hatred'. Dobrée's Wycherley is a precursor to August Strindberg: both dramatists tell uncomfortable truths about human sexuality and the desire for power. This view restored Wycherley's literary respectability but it undervalues his playfulness and compassion for his heroines.

Directors still have to decide on their version of Wycherley: the libertine, the creator of light comedies existing in a self-referential world, the moral satirist or a writer who eludes all these definitions.

Wycherley did not have Etherege's financial resources. He could not afford to be an amateur but he detested sycophancy. *The Plain Dealer* has a mock dedication to a notorious procuress, Mother Bennet, satirising the flattery that professional playwrights heaped on wealthy patrons. In his later years, after a serious illness, he suffered from a severely impaired memory and wrote no more plays. *Love in a Wood* (1671), *The Gentleman Dancing-Master* (1672), *The Country Wife* and *The Plain Dealer* all belong to the 1670s.

All four plays favour marriages based on love rather than arranged matches. Three of the four include scenes where the characters are misled in their sexual adventures by darkness, and all involve a character who claims to be somebody else. These shared traits suggest Wycherley's fascination with seeing clearly and showing how desire distorts our vision.

Love in a Wood attempts to include something to please everybody and so seems cumbersome. It has a heroic plot concerning the courageous Valentine and his faithful Christina; there is a comic intrigue involving the libertine Ranger and his mistress, Lydia; finally there is a satire on middle-class morality in which Dapperwit and Alderman Gripe compete for the favours of Lucy. Lucy is helped to make a profitable arrangement with Gripe by her mother and the bawd Mrs Joyner, who shares Gripe's hypocritical piety:

> Yesterday, as I told you, a fine old alderman of the city, seeing your daughter in so ill hands as Dapperwit's, was zealously, and in pure charity, bent upon her redemption; and has sent me to tell you, he will take her into his care and relieve your necessities.

Love in a Wood, an urban *A Midsummer Night's Dream*, is set around the 'forest' of St James' Park. In the second act, the park at night encourages a series of amorous misunderstandings and in the fifth a return to the park's darkness brings resolution. The reunited lovers celebrate their happiness in the adjoining Mulberry Gardens.

The Gentleman Dancing-Master is Wycherley's most explicit depiction of female sexuality. It has a likeable heroine but is too long for its thin plot. By avoiding the use of a subplot, Wycherley imitates European comedies (his play was inspired by Calderon's *El Maestro de Danzar*). It observes the three unities of time, place and action. This intensifies the claustrophobia of the heroine's surroundings and the urgency of her dilemma. James Formal adopts Spanish manners in London and reinvents himself as Don Diego. He educates his daughter Hippolita according to Spanish principles: she is restricted to her home and forbidden male company. Don Diego intends to marry her to his Francophile nephew, Mr Paris, but Hippolita is attracted to Gerrard, a 'young gentleman of the town'. She persuades him to pretend to be a dancing master, although he sings and dances poorly, so that she may talk to him and discover whether he will make a good husband.

Wycherley emphasises that Hippolita's interest in love is not simply related to one man but is part of her emerging sense of self. As a fourteen-year-old, instead of being restricted to the house, she should be discovering her instincts: how wrong it is, she exclaims, 'to confine a woman just in her rambling age!' Dobrée comments on the 'hatred Wycherley has for Hippolita because she has the desires natural to the animal'. But Wycherley makes an enlightened point about education: a repressed child does not become a saint, as Hippolita explains to her chaperone:

> **Hippolita:** I never lived so wicked a life as I have done this twelvemonth, since I have not seen a man.
> **Mrs Caution:** How, how! If you have not seen a man, how could you be wicked? How could you do any ill?
> **Hippolita:** I have done no ill; but I have paid it with thinking.

Hippolita takes the initiative. Given her father's insanity, she is risking her life: 'He might kill me as the shame and stain of his honour and his family.' She tests Gerrard through repeated encounters and humiliates him because 'passion unmasks every man.' Eventually she marries him, but she insists on 'plain dealing'. She sees male jealousy in marriage not as a proof of love but as an attempt to control women:

> **Hippolita:** So that upon the whole matter I conclude, jealousy in a gallant is humble true love, and the height of respect, and only an undervaluing of himself to overvalue her; but in a husband 'tis arrant sauciness, cowardice, and ill-breeding, and not to be suffered.
> **Gerrard:** I stand corrected, gracious miss.

Although *The Gentleman Dancing-Master* is a minor work, it is a first sketch of the themes and structural patterns of *The Country Wife*. The restrictive Don Diego and the complacent Mr Paris resemble Pinchwife and Sparkish. Hippolita, like Margery, opposes emotional honesty to social convention.

The Country Wife and *The Plain Dealer* are Wycherley's best-known works. Because they are based on plays by Molière, Wycherley is sometimes dismissed as a mere imitator or plagiarist. Macaulay says: 'There is hardly anything of the least value in his plays of which the hint is not to be found elsewhere.' Molière's *The School for Wives* (1662) and *The Misanthrope* (1666), the sources for *The Country Wife* and *The Plain Dealer* respectively, are masterpieces of French comedy so the argument is complicated by questions about whether Wycherley 'improved on' or travestied the earlier plays. Molière is lightly ironic while Wycherley is satirical. The equivalents of Margery and Olivia are unmarried in Molière's plays so that the issue of adultery, which so antagonises Macaulay, is less relevant. Arnolphe, like Pinchwife, is so afraid of being cuckolded that he plans to marry a girl of less than half his age, whom he can control. But Arnolphe is outwitted and Agnès marries the young Horace. Pinchwife and Margery remain trapped at the conclusion of *The Country Wife* in an unhappy marriage. Arnolphe is the guardian of his prospective wife and raises her in a way intended to guarantee her stupidity and docility; Margery is not stupid: she is naïve by London standards, but she belongs to a community with different values. Molière mocks attempts to shape women according to masculine ideals; Wycherley exposes the heartless artificiality of fashionable city life.

Wycherley intensifies the wrongdoings of his characters. The china scene in *The Country Wife* recalls an ambiguous discussion between Agnès and Arnolphe about a ribbon but the ambiguities work in opposite directions: Sir Jasper's remark through a closed door to his wife about Horner 'coming in to you the back way' may ironically describe a sexual position the unseen lovers are adopting but, in Molière, Arnolphe's suspicions are unfounded. Unlike Horner, Horace in *The School for Wives* is not a libertine: he is the generic young man (a *jeune premier*) who loves Agnès and marries her. Arnolphe never physically bullies Agnès, while Pinchwife threatens to disfigure Margery with a penknife. Equally, Célimène in *The Misanthrope,* unlike Olivia in *The Plain Dealer*, does not swindle the hero or marry his best friend.

Even its harshest critics have praised *The Country Wife* for its wit. For Macaulay, the play's polished style highlights its moral emptiness; it is 'one of the most profligate and heartless of human compositions'. Kenneth Tynan, in an *Observer* review (16th December 1956) of a Royal Court production, says approvingly that *The Country Wife* is 'about nothing but sex', but his praise of Joan Plowright's Margery (her 'child-bride is a gorgeous little goof, with a knowing slyness that perfectly matches her Rochdale accent') is a reminder that Wycherley is equally concerned with the different ways people speak and how they express their desires.

The wit in *The Country Wife* is expressed in pithy aphorisms or maxims. Pinchwife declares of his decision to marry an ignorant woman: ''Tis my maxim, he's a fool that marries; but he's a greater that does not marry a fool.' Horner and Dorilant compete to produce the sharpest maxim on a theme set by Harcourt:

> **Harcourt:** Most men are the contraries to that they would seem. Your bully, you see, is a coward with a long sword; the little humbly-fawning physician, with his ebony cane, is he that destroys men.
> **Dorilant:** The usurer, a poor rogue, possessed of mouldy bonds and mortgages; and we they call spendthrifts, are only wealthy, who lay out his money upon daily new purchases of pleasure.
> **Horner:** Ay, your arrantest cheat is your trustee or executor; your jealous man, the greatest cuckold; your churchman, the greatest atheist; and your noisy pert rogue of a wit, the greatest fop, dullest ass, and worst company, as you shall see; for here he comes. [*Enter* Sparkish.]

Horner is linguistically opposed to Sparkish. Horner is in complete command of his language. He never gives anything away unintentionally. Sparkish aspires to the same control but says more than he realises. He admits this after he declares his poor opinion of 'matrimonial love' before his fiancée, Alithea: 'I went too far ere I was aware.'

Horner's name denotes his function: he gives husbands their cuckolds' horns by seducing their wives. In *The Plain Dealer*, Olivia rightly mentions 'the clandestine obscenity in the very name of Horner'. His seductions shock not because of their bawdiness – popular farces such as D'Urfey's *The Fond Husband* (1677) were more explicit – but because they are gestures of contempt for the society which fosters him. He boasts, 'I am still on the criminal's side against the innocent'; in such a corrupt world, the terms 'criminal' and 'innocent' are reversible. By spreading the myth that he has been made impotent by a botched operation for the pox, he makes seduction easier but debars himself from a 'respectable' marriage. Considering the quality of the husbands around him, such as Sir Jasper and Pinchwife, he may have chosen the better alternative. Only his disinterested sorrow, on hearing that Harcourt has lost Alithea to Sparkish, humanises him.

Wycherley implies that ideals used in support of marriage, such as 'honour', are frauds in a society devoted to selfishness. It is this attack on cherished institutions, rather than his innuendoes about china, that made Wycherley into Macaulay's 'skunk'. Society is a game; the penalties for losing are severe; they include public disgrace and poverty. The counters Lady Fidget and her friends use to defend themselves are words like honour and virtue. Like chess pieces, these words have no innate value but they have great power in the game. Horner recognises this: 'Your women of honour, as you call 'em, are only chary of their reputations, not their persons; and 'tis scandal they would avoid, not men.' P.F. Vernon argues in *William Wycherley* (1965) that the irony is not only directed at women: 'Although he ridicules the pretended virtue of society ladies like Lady Fidget, Wycherley looks at them quite sympathetically. He shows that their deceitfulness develops naturally as a reaction to the cruelty and indifference of men.'

Lady Fidget's display of shock when her husband uses the word 'naked' in the phrase 'naked truth' illustrates the gulf between her private behaviour and public persona. When Mrs Sqeamish asserts that adultery is not so serious if undiscovered, Lady Fidget goes further, arguing that adultery is not shameful unless it is public knowledge:

Mrs Squeamish: The crime's the less serious when 'tis not known.
Lady Fidget: You say true; i'faith, I think you are in the right on't; 'tis not an injury to a husband, till it be an injury to our honours.

Margery, as a plain speaker, is placed in opposition to Lady Fidget. The comedy concerning Margery exposes her ignorance of social conventions but it also questions the value of those conventions. Lady Fidget and her friends maintain the appearance of fidelity to their husbands while they deceive them with Horner. Margery declares publicly that her marriage is unhappy and that she wishes to leave her husband for the man she loves. The other characters refuse to hear her. She complains in a letter to Horner:

I hope you will speedily find some way to free me from this unfortunate match, which was never, I assure you, of my choice, but I'm afraid 'tis already too far gone;

Letter writing is important in *The Country Wife*. Pinchwife makes Margery write by threatening her: 'Write as I bid you, or I will write whore with this penknife in your face.' But Margery soon expresses her own views rather than those of her husband. When women such as Aphra Behn were gaining literary reputations, Margery's letters become a significant gesture of intellectual independence.

If there is a hero in *The Country Wife*, it is Harcourt. He is faithful to Alithea while encouraging her to deceive Sparkish. Harcourt teaches the dangerous libertine lesson that we sometimes outgrow our promises. The jealous Pinchwife and the complacent Sparkish demand a similar level of ignorance in their wives. Sparkish does not care about his wife's behaviour as long as she is discreet and does not interfere with his own pleasures. Alithea eventually recognises the cold-heartedness under his pliant manner:

Alithea: You astonish me, sir, with your want of jealousy.
Sparkish: And you make me giddy, madam, with your jealousy and fears, and virtue and honour. 'Gad, I see virtue makes a woman as troublesome as a little reading or learning.
Alithea: Monstrous!

Alithea and Margery are taught emotional survival by Harcourt and Horner. As Simon Callow argues, 'The difference between teaching and corruption is quite a fine one.'

The Country Wife ends with 'A Dance of Cuckolds'. Dances sometimes conclude Elizabethan comedies to symbolise social harmony but Wycherley treats this convention ironically, suggesting that we dance together by ignoring the truths we do not wish to stumble over. *The Plain Dealer* is about a hero who refuses to join the dance. Different types of hypocrisy become Wycherley's subject. Lord Plausible's insincere compliments are contrasted with Novel's gratuitous rudeness; Olivia's infidelities are set against Fidelia's extreme devotion; Eliza's tolerance is balanced by the Widow Blackacre's litigiousness; Freeman's genuine friendship for Manly is the opposite of Vernish's pretence of friendship. These contrasts are not clear-cut. Olivia is hypocritical but Fidelia disguises herself as a man to join Manly at sea; both deceive him in different ways.

Manly arrives in London in near-poverty after a sea battle with the Dutch. As one of his sailors claims, 'He was resolved never to return again for England.' Manly, despising the hypocrisies of civilisation, intended to settle in the West Indies. He leaves his fortune with Olivia before sailing and expects her to join him once he has built a house. But Olivia secretly marries Vernish and refuses to return Manly's money. She falls in love with Fidelia (supposedly a man). Manly, after learning of Olivia's marriage, attempts to expose this adulterous passion. Vernish discovers his wife's feelings and Fidelia regains Manly's money. She then reveals that she is an heiress and marries Manly.

The Plain Dealer stretches the conventions of Restoration Comedy. Manly dismisses polite society as 'chattering baboons'. The harsh tone is increased by Wycherley's interest in 'railing' where *The Country Wife* relies on wit. Railing accumulates exaggerated abuse in an orgy of excess. Novel explains that it is a violent practice 'for railing is satire, you know; and roaring and making a noise, humour.'

The depiction of Olivia is troubling. She is a hypocritical thief but Wycherley humiliates her with relish. She speaks for the prudes who protested against his portrayal of women in *The Country Wife*. Olivia supposedly hates plays: 'I abominate 'em; filthy, obscene, hideous things.' She is however shrewd on Manly's masculine vanity: 'He that distrusts most the world, trusts most to himself, and is but the more easily deceived.' Olivia's hypocrisy may be more sympathetic than Manly's 'plain speaking'.

Olivia is contrasted with Fidelia, whose name symbolises her loyalty. Fidelia is a deliberately unrealistic character, borrowed from

Shakespeare's *Twelfth Night*. Critics have never believed in her but then Wycherley did not believe in her either. She offers a purely theatrical salvation for Manly, who would otherwise be doomed to poverty. As the prologue sarcastically asks:

> And where else, but on stages, do we see
> Truth pleasing, or rewarded honesty?

Freeman, a 'complier with the age', asks the most important question in Wycherley's play: 'Would you have a man speak truth to his ruin?' In later life, one of Wycherley's favourite books was the *Maxims* (1665) of the Duc de la Rochefoucauld. The most famous maxim (no. 218) could well apply to either of Wycherley's last plays: 'Hypocrisy is a sort of homage which vice pays to virtue.' Rochefoucauld's maxim 119 gives some insight into why Wycherley repeatedly created scenes where the characters flounder in darkness: 'We are so much in the habit of wearing disguises that we end by failing to recognise ourselves.'

5

The Cruel Fathers: Restoration Tragedy

Restoration tragedies are rarely performed today. Their stylised concentration on suffering alienates modern tastes. But these tragedies ask questions about morality and political authority with a surprising freedom and the monarchs portrayed are often unsympathetic characters. Boabdelin in Dryden's *The Conquest of Granada* (1670) loses his kingdom through petty-mindedness, Tarquin in *Lucius Junius Brutus* by Nathaniel Lee (1680) is a rapist, and the King of Spain, in Otway's *Don Carlos* (1676), marries his intended daughter-in-law and kills his son. Charles II came to see Dryden's *The Conquest of Granada* to admire his mistress Nell Gwyn in a starring role but he heard a player-king denounce monarchy as a system based on coercive power: ''Tis true from force the noblest title springs;/I therefore hold from that, which first made kings.' Neither Dryden nor Charles shared this view but the one wrote the speech and the other tranquilly listened.

Dr Johnson in his 'Life of Dryden' argues that the poet reluctantly wrote plays, 'compelled undoubtedly by necessity'. Dryden's contemporaries disagreed. Nathaniel Lee collaborated with him; Southerne and Congreve regarded him as their mentor while Buckingham parodied him in *The Rehearsal* (1671) because he was England's leading dramatist.

Dryden is easy to mock for his inconsistencies. In *Of Dramatick Poesie* (1668), he compares Shakespeare and Jonson and decides he prefers Shakespeare. He later thought he had underrated Jonson. His critical judgements were always provisional. *Of Dramatick Poesie* begins with an admission: 'I find many things in this Discourse which I do not now approve; my judgment being not a little altered since the writing of it; but whether for the better or the worse, I know not.'

No other Restoration dramatist matches Dryden's versatility. In a career of forty years he created an influential comedy of manners with *Marriage à la Mode* (1673), heroic dramas such as *Aureng-Zebe*

(1675) and farces including *The Kind Keeper* (1679). He provocatively re-imagines the work of previous playwrights. *All for Love* (1677) is not an adaptation of Shakespeare's *Antony and Cleopatra* but a complex response to it. *Oedipus* (1679) explores the tragedy that Aristotle argued was a perfect model of the genre. *Amphitryon*, written in 1690 after the overthrow of James II and his replacement by William and Mary as joint sovereigns, reworks a classical legend to question the theory of the divine right of kings.

Dryden established his reputation with heroic dramas in the early 1670s. Such plays exalt virtue and extreme emotion. In the dedication to the first part of *The Conquest of Granada*, he claims that the 'kind of poesy, which excites to virtue the greatest men is of the greatest use to humankind'. The hero is unambiguously good, even if over-impetuous: 'I designed in him a roughness of character, impatient of injuries.' This protagonist faces a basic conflict of loyalty. Women are self-sacrificing angels or sultry temptresses. The hero or heroine's true parentage may be concealed. The action is accompanied by stirring music.

Dobrée in his *John Dryden* (1956; revised 1961) admits: 'The heroic drama of the Restoration period is a glorious extravaganza written for a special audience: to enjoy it today … is perhaps to indulge an acquired vice.' Heroic drama anticipates fantasy and action movies, in which characterisation is minimal and improbable storylines are accompanied by an emphatic soundtrack. The first *Star Wars* trilogy includes such heroic drama traits as clear-cut heroes and villains, self-sacrifice, spectacle and revelations about the hero's parentage.

In *The Conquest of Granada*, Dryden depicts the end of Moorish rule in Spain in 1492. His Moors defeat themselves through clan rivalries. The Christian besiegers are rarely seen. Almanzor is an Achilles figure with an absolute conception of personal honour but Lyndaraxa is the more interesting character. Her ruthless determination to become a queen gives her a comic resourcefulness. Her death is moving because she does not die nobly. Stabbed by one of her lovers, she refuses to believe that she will never achieve her ambition: 'Destiny mistakes; this death's not mine.'

Dryden's finest plays are *Marriage à la Mode*, *All for Love* and *Amphitryon*. The song at the beginning of *Marriage à la Mode* captures a key theme of Restoration Comedy:

Why should a foolish marriage vow
Which long ago was made,
Oblige us to each other now
When passion is decayed?

The comic plot of the play turns on the loss of sexual desire in marriage. Rhodophil is unhappily married to Doralice; Palamede is engaged to the pretentious Melantha. Rhodophil falls in love with Melantha while Palamede and Doralice are attracted. The play recounts the foursome's efforts to consummate their illicit loves. Romantic clichés are treated with urbane irony:

> **Doralice:** If you had stayed a minute longer, I was just considering whether I should stab, hang, or drown myself.

The humour is founded on a marital unhappiness which is even conveyed in stage directions. Doralice and Rhodophil 'walk contrary ways on the stage: he, with his hands in his pocket, whistling; she, singing a dull melancholy tune.' Palamede eventually asks whether they should form 'a blessed community betwixt us four, for the solace of women, and relief of men', but they decide that this community would fall apart through jealousy and that it is better to stay monogamous.

This 'happy' ending follows several bleak reflections on desire. Doralice compares sex to eating and complains of the men: 'Because they cannot feed on one dish, therefore we must be starved.' Rhodophil argues that variety enlivens marriage: 'A sweet mistress now and then, makes my sweet lady so much more sweet.' Palamede describes the attraction of masquerades, leading to anonymous encounters: 'The bold discoverer leaps ashore, and takes his lot among the wild Indians and savages, without the vile consideration of safety to his person, or of bounty or wholesomeness in his mistress.' The risk of infection from an 'unwholesome' mistress only adds to the thrill. Palamede suggests a mechanistic view of desire: 'We move and talk just like so many over-grown puppets.'

In *Marriage à la Mode*'s heroic plot the tyrant Polydamus is deposed by Leonidas. Polydamus finds his conqueror so admirable that he exclaims:

O, had I known you could have been this king.
Thus god-like, great and good, I should have wished
T'have been dethroned before.

Is the absurdity intentional? Leonidas' heroism is as unconvincing as the reconciliation of the four lovers.

In his dedication to *The Spanish Friar* (1680), Dryden claims "Tis more difficult to save than 'tis to kill.' He was temperamentally opposed to ending a play in devastation. In his Preface to *All for Love*, he complains of the limitations imposed by his historical source: 'That which is wanting to work up the pity to a greater height; was not afforded by the story.' Conversely, he distorts history to allow a confrontation between Antony's wife, Octavia, and Cleopatra. The tragic ending and the undignified rivalry between Octavia and Cleopatra, give the play two of its strengths. A third is the use of the three unities to increase the tension as Octavius' unseen legions approach the palace.

In the first act, Antony recalls a dream which suggests Dryden's archetypal approach:

Stretched at my length beneath some blasted oak,
I lean my hand upon the mossy bark,
And look just of a piece as I grew from it;
My uncombed locks matted by mistletoe
Hung o'er my hoary face; a murm'ring brook
Runs at my foot.

There is a death wish in Antony's dissolution into the natural world. The oak and the mistletoe are strangely Nordic symbols for a Roman to dream of in Egypt. The god murdered by mistletoe is Balder, the Norse god of light. Antony is out of place in his own tragedy; he is a setting northern sun in a world of Mediterranean power politics.

The worldly Cleopatra evokes the heroines of Restoration comedy. On her first appearance, she despises 'respectable' wives:

Respect is for a wife: Am I that thing,
That dull, insipid lump, without desires,
And without power to give them?

Her journey is towards a mystical marriage with Antony. In Act IV, she laments: 'Nature meant me/A wife; a silly, harmless, household dove.' As she kills herself, she vows:

> My nobler fate
> Shall knit our spousals with a tie, too strong
> For Roman law to break.

She supplants Octavia as Antony's 'true' wife. Octavia undertakes the opposite journey, away from Antony and marriage. On her first entrance, 'leading Antony's two little daughters', she asserts her moral authority as a wife and mother. She offers reconciliation, poignantly suggesting that Antony may abandon her after making peace with her brother:

> He shall draw back his troops, and you shall march
> To rule the East: I may be dropt at Athens,
> No matter where.

Octavia urges her children to reclaim Antony: 'Pull him to yourselves, from that bad woman.' In her confrontation with Cleopatra, she makes the mistake of abandoning her dignity. She discovers that 'bad women' are often better at arguing than virtuous ones:

> **Octavia:** Shame of our sex,
> Dost thou not blush to own those black endearments,
> That make sin pleasing.
> **Cleopatra:** You may blush who want them.

Octavia denounces Cleopatra to Antony as a 'faithless prostitute' and so pushes her wavering husband to the Queen's side. Octavia's tragedy is that she begins with a grand gesture and then recognises her own triviality. *All for Love* has a comic side. The lovers are driven to their tragic end by a series of bungling attempts to divide them.

Amphitryon is Dryden's most melancholic drama. He depicts the destruction of human happiness at the whim of absolute power. Jupiter, king of the gods, decides to have sex with Amphitryon's wife, Alcmena. This will lead to the conception of Hercules. Amphitryon is returning home from war. Jupiter appears in the guise of the husband and so forestalls him. He is assisted by Mercury, the god of trickery, disguised as Sosia, Amphitryon's slave. Jupiter claims he is the embodiment of divine will:

> Fate is, what I
> By virtue of omnipotence have made it;
> And power omnipotent can do no wrong.

Mercury is unimpressed: 'Here's omnipotence with a vengeance – to make a man a cuckold, and yet not to do him wrong.'

Plautus and Molière in their versions of the myth emphasise Amphitryon's confusion on discovering he has been cuckolded. Dryden expands Alcmena's role. She complains to the disguised Jupiter, one of those 'niggard gods' who make love a rarity:

> Ye niggard gods, you make our lives too long.
> You fill 'em with diseases, wants and woes,
> And only dash'em with a little love,
> Sprinkled by fits, and with a sparing hand.

Jupiter becomes the victim of his own deception through his refusal to believe that Alcmena's love-making was intended for her husband. The great seducer complains of the limitations of the sexual act: 'The common love of sex to sex is brutal.' When Alcmena realises she has been tricked she is inconsolable: 'A simple error is a real crime; / And unconsenting innocence is lost.'

Mercury declares: 'Our Jupiter is a great comedian; he counterfeits most admirably.' This reminds us that we are watching a comedy, based on jokes of mistaken identity and cuckoldry, but who is laughing at the end? Jupiter finally orders the married couple to be happy in their fulfilment of providence. Alcmena and Amphitryon remain silent.

Dryden's collaboration with Nathaniel Lee produced some distinctive work. Their *Oedipus* (1678) is an adaptation of a venerated text. In their preface, the authors emphasise that Sophocles' play 'was the most celebrated Piece of all Antiquity'. They depart from Sophocles in the creation of a subplot, which they regard as essential to an English play: 'Custom likewise has obtained, that we must form an Under-plot of second Persons, which must be depending on the first, and their By-walks must be like those in a Labyrinth, which all of 'em lead into the great Parterre.' The architectural metaphor of a labyrinth reveals an aesthetic in which complexity is preferred to simplicity. Sophocles' play offers a remorseless single progression of events to an inescapable climax; Dryden and Lee create a tangled drama of persecuted love and political intrigue in which Oedipus' incestuous marriage seems incidental.

Dryden and Lee refashion *Oedipus* in Shakespearean terms. Creon, like Richard III, is a hunchbacked usurper. There are references to *Macbeth*, including a conjuration: 'The Ghost of Laius rises arm'd in his Chariot as he was slain.' Jocasta is conflated with Medea when she murders her children: 'Scene draws and discovers Jocasta held by her Women, and stab'd in many Places of her Bosom, her Hair disshevel'd; her Children slain upon the Bed.' This adaptation suggests an ambition among the Restoration playwrights which has long been underrated.

If Dryden occupied the centre of the literary world, Lee and Otway were tragic outsiders. Both were stage-struck university students and unsuccessful actors. Otway died penniless in his early thirties, Lee died in his forties after a struggle against insanity. Unlike most Restoration tragedians, Lee had no interest in 'classical restraint'. A dragon appears in *The Rival Queens* (1677), and in *Lucius Junius Brutus* priests support the rapist King Tarquin by flaying men alive. Lee's bombastic style is sometimes associated with his madness but it is a deliberate literary choice. He is interested in extremes of self-indulgence and self-discipline.

In *The Rival Queens,* Alexander the Great is placed between Roxana and Statira, who respectively represent erotic passion and high-minded devotion. After Statira leaves her unfaithful husband to retire to 'the bowers of great Semiramis', Roxana taunts her with the love-making that will go on in her absence:

> Thou shalt see,
> Through the drawn curtains, that great man and me,
> Wearied with laughing joys.

Although Alexander loves Statira, his behaviour is as excessive as Roxana's. He claims to be a god, giving his irrational actions a divine authority. In excusing his love-making with Roxana, he associates sex with his destruction of a city; both happened when he was drunk and he was sorry afterwards.

But when I waked, I shook the Circe off,
Though that enchantress held me by the arm,
And wept, and gazed with all the force of love;
Nor grieved I less for that which I had done,
Than when at Thais' suit, enraged with wine,
I set the famed Persepolis on fire.

Lee's vision of Alexander and his queens has a parodic subtext: despite their long declarations of love, all three are self-obsessed. In his adaptation of Lee's play, *Alexander the Great* (1796), the actor John Philip Kemble has Thessalus hear 'Ammon's voice' in Alexander's death cries. Perhaps Kemble introduces this detail to counterbalance Alexander's egomania: the mad king really is the son of a god.

Lucius Junius Brutus was suppressed because the hero's republican speeches were thought by the government to be too convincing. In Act I Lucrece, who has been raped by King Tarquin, commits suicide. As she dies, she demands vengeance. Brutus, who has feigned stupidity to avoid persecution, galvanises Rome with republican feeling: 'Swear from this time never to suffer them, / Nor any other king, to reign in Rome.' The vow is taken over Lucrece's body. Although Brutus leads the republican cause, Venditius makes the most persuasive arguments in a prose which recalls Commonwealth pamphlets: 'Why should any one man have more power than the people? Has he more guts or more brains than the people? What can he do for the people that the people can't do for themselves?'

Tiberius warns against government by an impersonal authority – by contrast, kings can show mercy: 'O, 'tis dangerous/To have all actions judged by rigorous law.' Both sides, however, are merciless. Tarquin's priests sacrifice republicans: 'The scene draws showing the sacrifice: one burning and another crucified; the Priests coming forward with goblets in their hands, filled with human blood.' Brutus has his two sons executed because they attempt to betray the republic. He prides himself on his 'rigorous Roman resolution' but he reveals a canny awareness of public opinion. Nothing plays to the crowd like integrity. His vision of an incorruptible Rome is a totalitarian state:

Vagabonds, walkers, drones, and swarming braves,
The froth of states, scummed from the commonwealth,
Idleness banished, all excess repressed.

Lee's last singly authored play, *The Princess of Cleves* (1681), is based on Madame de La Fayette's novel about a marital triangle between three morally scrupulous individuals. Lee parodies La Fayette's values. He turns Nemours into a libertine, as he boasts in his dedication: 'They expected the most polished hero in Nemours, I gave 'em a ruffian'. Rochester died while Lee was writing the play; the laments of the libertines for Count Rosidore are ambivalent tributes to the Earl. Nemours' praise of Rosidore is revealing: 'He never spoke a witty thing twice.' Repetition in words or women makes for boredom: 'In a domestic she, there's no gaity, no chat, no discourse ... my thing asked me once, when my breeches were down, what the stuff cost a yard.'

Despite his libertine views, Nemours hesitates between Marguerite, who shows him new erotic pleasures when he is about to discard her, and the Princess. The Princess is faithful to her invalid husband but has an orgasmic dream about Nemours:

> I found a pleasure I ne'er felt before,
> Dissolving pains, and swimming, shuddering joys,
> To which my bridal night with Cleves was dull.

Cleves' awareness of his wife's desires hastens his death from a weak heart. Nemours exhibits both compassion (he weeps for the dying man) and bare-faced opportunism as he attempts to seduce the grieving widow in 'the undress of her soul'. After a final confrontation with the Princess, Nemours decides to marry Marguerite. This play is the most subtle of Lee's tragedies. It ends with its hero in mental collapse, trying to adopt an attitude (cynical libertine or repentant husband?) to withstand an emotional onslaught which transcends his philosophy.

Samuel Johnson calls Thomas Otway 'one of the first names in English drama'. Otway's dedications and prologues proclaim his Stuart loyalties but the plays are more subversive than their author. His protagonists are repressed by their reactionary elders. In *Don Carlos* (1676) Philip II marries the princess intended for his son. In *The Soldier's Fortune* (1680) Sir Davy Dunce marries Beaugard's beloved while he is abroad serving his country. Another soldier, Pierre, in *Venice Preserved*, finds that his mistress has been seduced by Senator Antonio, while Jaffier's wife is almost raped by the aged revolutionary Renault. Acasto in *The Orphan* (1680) shields his twin sons from the corruption of the court by forcing them to stay at home. The result is an incestuous tragedy of frustrated desire.

Otway's plays have such a thematic unity that the terms tragedy and comedy are barely applicable. His comedies, *Friendship in Fashion* (1678), *The Soldier's Fortune* and its sequel *The Atheist* (1683), have bleak conclusions. His tragedy *The Orphan* concerns a practical joke which goes wrong. Johnson deplores the 'despicable scenes of vile comedy' in *Venice Preserved*, which portray Antonio's advances to his mistress. But when Antonio tempts Aquilano with purses of gold he reiterates a message which pervades the plays: the old men have the power and they are killing their sons.

Otway's interest in subverting dramatic genres dates from 1677, when he translated Racine's *Bérénice* (1670). The choice of this play is significant: it is a tragedy which does not end with a death. Racine argued that the lifelong separation of two lovers is a tragic conclusion. Otway's work also challenges the audience's expectations. In her introduction to *Four Restoration Libertine Plays* (2005) Deborah Payne Fisk praises *Friendship in Fashion* as a 'neglected masterpiece' and compares its portrayal of a disintegrating marriage to Edward Albee's *Who's Afraid of Virginia Woolf* (1962). In *Friendship and Fashion*, Goodvile organises a party to dispose of his pregnant mistress by marrying her to a friend. The central three acts depict the party and its unpleasant guests in gruelling detail. Wycherley had evoked Restoration wit at its sharpest, Otway portrays its sadistic side:

> **Malagene:** Why, walking along, a lame fellow followed me and asked my charity, which, by the way, was a pretty proposition to me. Being in one of my witty, merry fits, I asked him how long he had been in that condition. The poor fellow shook his head and told me he was born so. But how d'ye think I served him?
> **Valentine:** Nay, the devil knows.
> **Malagene:** I showed my parts, I think; for I tripped up both his wooden legs and walked off gravely about my business.
> **Valentine:** And this, you say, is your way of wit?

Goodvile's marriage breaks up, and the fifth act degenerates into a squabble over property. The announcement of the marriage of two secondary characters so that this 'comedy' can end in a traditional way is a cynical gesture. The most haunting moment is when Malagene 'sings an Irish cronan'; while this lament lasts a sorrow is expressed far beyond the emotional reach of these fashionable, self-centred people.

The Soldier's Fortune is similarly sombre. Beaugard and Courtine are two soldiers impoverished by serving the King abroad, while their less heroic countrymen have become wealthy by staying at home. Beaugard discovers that his true love has married the merchant, Sir Davy Dunce. Lady Dunce's friend, Sylvia, derides marriage to a much older man: 'to lie all night by a horse-load of diseases – a beastly, unsavoury, old, groaning, grunting, wheezing wretch'. Lady Dunce had married under pressure from her parents. She feels emotionally detached from her wedding vows: 'My parents indeed made me say something to him after a priest once, but my heart went not along with my tongue.' Lady Dunce and Beaugard are reunited with the help of the prurient and voyeuristic Sir Jolly Jumble, who wishes to watch their sexual encounters. Her bedroom eventually promises to be crowded, containing her senile husband, her lover and Sir Jolly. This is a travesty of a happy ending.

Don Carlos reveals Otway's tragic preoccupations most starkly. The older characters, such as the King and the Machiavellian Ruy-Gomez are corrupt and set out to dispossess the younger generation. The King has married the bride intended for his son, Don Carlos. Ruy-Gomez is deceived by his young wife, the Duchess of Eboli. The ensuing power struggle is rich in incestuous undertones. Don Carlos loves his stepmother and is murdered by his father. The Queen, Duchess and Ruy-Gomez are killed and the King goes mad. Liberty, joy and youth are murdered by the law, tyranny and age. It is a pattern which recurs in *The Orphan* and *Venice Preserved*.

The Orphan is set in and around Acasto's castle in Bohemia. Acasto has forbidden his sons, Castalio and Polydore from leaving their home because he detests the corruption of life at court. The twins are both attracted to Monimia, an orphan under Acasto's guardianship. Castalio secretly marries her and arranges to visit her room. To avoid detection, their wedding night must be enjoyed in silence and darkness. Polydore, though unaware of the marriage, learns of the intended meeting. He causes Castalio to be delayed and takes his place in Monimia's bed as a practical joke on his brother.

When the truth is discovered the three find themselves in a private hell. Monimia and Polydore have unwittingly committed not only adultery but also (according to seventeenth-century values) incest. Had Castalio and Monimia not concealed their marriage, or had Polydore not been unscrupulous, there would have been no crisis. Conversely, if they had shared a less inflexible moral code, they might have survived and even found happiness but they regard death as their only escape from dishonour.

The Orphan is an uneven play governed by the logic of nightmares. It begins with some clumsy expository dialogue, in which two courtiers exchange information already known to both of them. This opening establishes a ritualistic tone, preparing the audience for the deliberately unrealistic tragedy that follows. Monimia's brother Chamont recalls the experiences which cause his unexpected arrival at the castle and which occupy a landscape of prophecy and intuition:

Chamont: My bed shook under me, the curtain started,
And to my tortured fancy there appeared
The form of thee thus beauteous as thou art,
Thy garments flowing loose, and in each hand
A wanton lover, which by turns caressed thee
With all the freedom of unbounded pleasure.
I snatched my sword, and in the very moment
Darted it at the phantom – straight it left me –
Then rose and called for lights, when, oh, dire omen!
I found my weapon had the arras pierced
Just where the famous tale was interwoven
How th'unhappy Theban slew his father.
Monimia: And for this cause my virtue is suspected!
Because in dreams your fancy has been ridden,
I must be tortured waking!
Chamont: Have a care,
Labour not to be justified too fast;
Hear all, and then let justice hold the scale.
What followed was the riddle that confounds me:
Through a close lane, as I pursued my journey,
And meditated on the last night's vision,
I spied a wrinkled hag, with age grown double,
Picking dry sticks, and mumbling to herself.
Her eyes with scalding rheum were galled and red,
Cold palsy shook her head, her hands seemed withered,
And on her crooked shoulder she had wrapped
The tattered remnant of an old stripped hanging,
Which served to keep her carcass from the cold;
So there was nothing of a piece about her.
Her lower weeds were all o'er coarsely patched

With different rags, black, red, white, yellow,
And seemed to speak variety of wretchedness.
I asked her of my way, which she informed me;
Then craved my charity, and bade me hasten
To save a sister: at that word I started.

Chamont absurdly upbraids Monimia for his nightmare and the encounter that followed. Yet in Otway's dream-like world, Chamont is wise to trust his intuition. His mention of 'th'unhappy Theban' is a reference to Oedipus and places *The Orphan* in the tradition of incest tragedy. In *Sweet Violence: The Idea of the Tragic* (2003), Terry Eagleton argues that in its subversion of the societal values surrounding marriage, incest is 'a kind of radical politics in itself'. By fusing the absurdity of the practical joke with the gravity of tragedy, *The Orphan* is radical in ways which are still disturbing.

Venice Preserved was written at the time of 'the 'Popish plot' and explores the social panic caused by the presumed threat to national security. Otway describes this paranoia in his prologue:

In these distracted times, when each man dreads
The bloody stratagems of busy heads;
When we have feared, three years we know not what …

For close on 150 years, ever since Henry VIII's break with the Roman Catholic Church in the 1530s, England had intermittently felt threatened by the danger of an attempt to re-impose papal authority. The fear of Catholicism increased during Charles II's reign as it became clear that he would have no legitimate Protestant son and would therefore be succeeded by his Catholic brother, the Duke of York, later James.

This was the background to the Popish plot crisis. In 1678 rumours began to circulate that leading Roman Catholics were planning to assassinate the King. Titus Oates, an ex-Jesuit, swore an affidavit before a magistrate to the effect that he had attended a Jesuit meeting in France at which the plans had been agreed. Those implicated included the Queen herself, who was said to be plotting with her doctor to poison the King.

Oates was a fraud and the King, who interviewed him privately, caught him out in a number of lies but he was widely believed. No one was safe from suspicion. Anyone could be a crypto-Catholic and planning murder. Eventually Oates was arrested, tried for sedition and imprisoned. But the crisis had created a poisonous atmosphere of distrust.

In *Venice Preserved* the political motivations of the characters are ambiguous. The conspirators aim to destroy a corrupt senate but they may be equally corrupt. Belvidera, the heroine, apparently speaks for reason, urging that gradual change is better than bloodshed, but she may just as well represent an unthinking, self-interested conservatism. If the revolution succeeds, it is doubtful that it will benefit the people. The lecherous Antonio and the spiteful Priuli would be replaced by the lecherous and spiteful Renault. In performance, the actors playing the senators might double as the conspirators, exploiting a theatrical convention to imply that there is little to choose between the two sides.

Pierre embodies the noblest possibilities of revolution. Like Beaugard from *The Soldier's Fortune*, he is a soldier who discovers that the woman he loves has betrayed him in his absence. But he refuses to resume his relationship with his former mistress. He is a moral absolutist, declaring that he has 'lived in moral justice towards all men'. He regards the Church as an enforcer of political conservatism and derides its demand that he repent: 'I have searched that conscience, / And find no record there of crimes that scare me.'

Otway remained popular into the nineteenth century. His plays, especially *Don Carlos* and *Venice Preserved*, appealed alike to Romantic radicalism and Victorian liberalism. In a journal entry for 14th April 1814, Lord Byron appreciatively quotes one of Pierre's anticlerical speeches ('What whining monk art thou – what holy cheat?'). This staunchly royalist playwright did more than any other seventeenth-century English writer except John Milton to give revolutionaries of over two hundred years a lyrical voice.

6

Aphra Behn and the Masculine Part

Aphra Behn is probably the most frequently discussed of the Restoration dramatists. As the first professional woman playwright, she interests feminists and post-feminists. Her journey to the slave colony in Surinam, which inspired the novel *Oroonoko*, and her posthumously staged *The Widow Ranter* (1689), the first play set in an American colony, make her an important figure in colonial studies. Her biographers often reveal an ideological bias. Montague Summers, who edited her collected works in 1915, was a pioneering sexologist and mainly interested in her treatment of female desire. George Woodcock's *The English Sappho* concentrated on her as, simultaneously, a staunch supporter of the Stuarts, and a revolutionary writer. Maureen Duffy's *The Passionate Shepherdess* (1977) focuses on Behn's subversion of gender roles.

Accusations of plagiarism against Behn were particularly savage. These attacks had a misogynistic element. According to Maureen Duffy, 'The argument was a circular one: if a woman wrote it, it can't be very good and if it's any good a woman can't have written it.'

In her preface to *The Lucky Chance* (1686), Behn argues that, although she inhabits a female body, her creative power is her 'Masculine Part': 'All I ask, is the Privilege for my Masculine Part, the Poet in me ... to tread in those successful Paths my Predecessors have so long thriv'd in.' Since a 'masculine part' is also a penis, her claim to equal consideration has a satirical edge.

Throughout her plays, Behn likes extravagant action. Sword fights are frequent and there is a delight in spectacle, such as Angellica's advertising campaign in *The Rover* (1677). Although Behn uses the fixed scenery of the Restoration theatre, her stagecraft evokes the flexibility of Elizabethan staging where characters take the locations with them. The battle in the fourth act of *Abdelazer* (1676) is conveyed in seven fast-moving episodes which recall the battle scenes in *Antony and Cleopatra*. She celebrates the theatricality of the theatre.

The Turkish seraglio in *The False Count* (1681) is an illusion created to fool Francisco and Isabella, and *The Lucky Chance* includes a masque of dancing 'spirits'.

The comedies fall into two categories. Firstly, there are the emotional dramas inspired by Beaumont and Fletcher, which are comedies only in that they end with marriages rather than deaths. Her first two plays, *The Forc'd Marriage* (1670), in which the heroine is strangled by her husband but survives, and *The Amorous Prince* (1671), in which a husband employs his friend to test his wife's virtue, explore the anxieties and potential for violence in marriage. Her masterpiece in this series is *The Town Fop* (1676). Bellmour is forced to marry Diana rather than the woman he loves. Although he initially defies his guardian, Plotwell, he gives in to threats of impoverishment and prison. He fails to consummate the marriage, and, sick with self-loathing, resorts to a brothel. Here he encounters Betty Flauntit. Bellmour is sickened by the repulsiveness of sex without love ('What an odious thing mere Coupling is!'), while Betty makes a cool professional assessment: 'I hope he has his Maidenhead; if so, and rich too, Oh, what a booty were this for me!' Behn often portrays extremely narrow escapes from an unhappy union. In *The Forc'd Marriage*, *The Town Fop* and *The Lucky Chance* there is a failure to consummate a marriage leading to divorce and another, happier wedding.

Secondly, Behn wrote tightly-plotted situation comedies, usually involving the marital triangle of old husband, young wife and lover derived from the conventions of Italian *commedia dell'arte*. Her old men are Pantaloons, Willmore disguises himself as the Doctor in *The Rover, Part Two* (1681), a Harlequin and Scaramouche appear in the same play and *The Emperor of the Moon* (1687) adapts a French *commedia dell'arte* text. Conversely, her servants are among the most realistically drawn in Restoration drama. Moretta in *The Rover* sees through Willmore with an older woman's bitter clarity. Her counter-part, Petronella, in the *The Rover, Part Two*, advises La Nuche to avoid Willmore because 'poverty's catching.' There is a similar realism in *Abdelazer* when a soldier undermines the rhetoric of his superiors by declaring 'I have a Wife and Children; and if I die they beg.'

Behn's most significant plays include *The Amorous Prince*, *Abdelazer*, *The Rover*, *The Lucky Chance* and *The Widow Ranter*. *The Amorous Prince* portrays physical violence between lovers and gender confusions which recall Beaumont and Fletcher's *Philaster* (1609). Prince Frederick, a libertine, finally achieves emotional maturity and marries Cloris, whom he had seduced before the play begins. The subplot, in which Antonio tests his wife's fidelity by persuading his friend, Alberto, to court her, reveals Behn's interest in the complexities of desire. Alberto falls in love with the woman he believes to be Antonio's wife and suffers from his divided loyalties; his beloved is actually Antonio's unmarried sister-in-law. Antonio tests his wife to vindicate his latent homosexuality. If women are universally unfaithful, he may find 'satisfaction' with a male friend:

> **Alberto:** But what if I prevail, Antonio?
> **Antonio:** Then I'll renounce my faith in womankind.
> And place my satisfaction in thy Amity.

Homosexuality becomes an explicit theme when another courtier, Lorenzo, sees Cloris dressed as a boy and ponders soliciting 'him':

> 'Tis a fine Lad, how plump and white he is;
> Would I could meet him somewhere i'th'dark,
> I'd have a fling at him.

Abdelazer also evokes erotic obsessions. It is close in its treatment of race and dramatic scope to Shakespeare's *Titus Andronicus*; Abdelazer and Queen Isabella recall Aaron and Queen Tamora. Both queens are seductive older women who veer between murderous rage and lust. While Tamora is protective towards her sons, Isabella is complicit in the murder of her eldest and falsely claims that her second son is illegitimate to discredit his claim to the throne. Both Aaron and Abdelazer are black outsiders. Behn expands on Shakespeare's exploration of the erotic appeal of mixed-race relationships. Abdelazer boasts of his skilful love-making to the young heroine, Leonora:

> The Lights put out, thou in my naked Arms
> Wilt find me soft and smooth as polish'd Ebony;
> And all my Kisses on thy balmy Lips as sweet,
> As are the Breezes, breath'd amidst the Groves
> Of ripening Spices in the height of Day.

The Rover is perhaps Behn's finest play. Popular with King Charles and his brother, the Duke of York, who looked back to their exile during the Commonwealth with nostalgia, it was based on the unperformed play, *Thomaso*, by Thomas Killigrew, written in 1655. The Royal Shakespeare Company's revival of *The Rover* in 1986 was instrumental in a reassessment of Behn's reputation but John Barton's 'Director's Note' in the programme book suggests his reservations about its structure and themes:

> The alterations I have made are partly to streamline our version and help to clarify a confusing plot. The most obvious change is the turning of Belvile into a black soldier of fortune, and the setting of the play in a Spanish colony rather than in Spain. I have however, deliberately avoided naming a specific location. The most obvious addition is that Valeria is introduced earlier in the action. Aphra Behn seems to regard her as an important engine of the plot, but does not have her speak until well into the play. The scene between Blunt and Lucetta is now closer to *Thomaso* than *The Rover* […] Angellica's part has been expanded in the first half.

Some of Barton's decisions are attractive but Belvile's change into a 'black soldier of fortune' is more controversial. This may be a pragmatic decision, made so that Hugh Quarshie might take the part. Belvile is an important agent of the Stuart government in exile, however, and this political dimension is lost. Barton's most troubling decision is to relocate the drama. Behn's location is not Spain, as Barton claims, but the Spanish-occupied Italian city of Naples. The play depicts the uneasy interaction between three distinct groups: the Spanish conquerors, the conquered Italians and the English cavaliers.

The alternative title of *The Rover* is *The Banish'd Cavaliers* – that is, the Englishmen who, out of loyalty to the Stuarts, have accepted exile and the probable confiscation of their lands rather than submission to the Commonwealth. It is a noble gesture with squalid results. The cavaliers are impoverished mercenaries. In a society dominated by rank, they elude classification: they are landless landowners, patriots without a country and men of honour available to be hired cheaply. Like the prostitutes that surround them, they also hire out their bodies.

Angellica is a key figure in the play. There is a kinship between the theatre and her advertising campaign, which is not based on any sexual expertise but on spectacle, mystery and social status. In his first confrontation with her, Willmore challenges this strategy:

Moretta: He knows himself of old, I believe those Breeches and he have been acquainted ever since he was beaten at Worcester.

Angellica: Nay, do not abuse the poor Creature. –

Moretta: Good Weather-beaten Corporal, will you march off? we have no need of your Doctrine, tho you have of our Charity; but at present we have no Scraps, we can afford no kindness for God's sake; in fine, Sirrah, the Price is too high i'th'Mouth for you, therefore troop, I say.

Willmore: Here, good Fore-Woman of the Shop, serve me, and I'll be gone.

Moretta: Keep it to pay your Landress, your Linen stinks of the Gun-Room; for here's no selling by Retail.

Willmore: Thou hast sold plenty of thy stale Ware at a cheap Rate.

Moretta: Ay, the more silly kind Heart I, but this is an Age wherein Beauty is at higher Rates. – In fine, you know the price of this.

Willmore: I grant you 'tis here set down at a thousand Crowns a Month – Baud, take your black Lead and sum it up, that I may have a Pistole-worth of these vain gay things, and I'll trouble you no more.

Willmore's teasing is based on a bawdy premise: if it costs a thousand Crowns to hire Angellica for a month, what specific service can be got for some loose change? But Angellica does not sell 'by Retail'; she sells status. The man that affords her will be powerful and enviable. Moretta and Willmore shrewdly identify each other's weaknesses. Moretta may have been a courtesan like Angellica but she is now old and cannot sell her 'stale Ware'. Willmore is a gentleman and a captain but he is so poor that he could as well be a 'weather-beaten Corporal'. The Civil War battle at Worcester (3rd September 1651) was a final, decisive defeat for the Royalists. Angellica says little during this extract. Although she is in authority, both Moretta and Willmore refer to her as a commodity: 'the price of this'. But she is attracted to Willmore. The night ends with an ironic reversal of her usual dealings with men: she gives him money.

Like Mrs Loveit in Etherege's *The Man of Mode*, Angellica is humiliated in the last act and abandoned by her lover for an heiress. But while Mrs Loveit is histrionic, Angellica reveals a moving vulnerability. The audience doubts that Willmore has made the right choice. Behn's sequel, *The Rover, Part Two*, reverses his earlier decision. With Hellena dead, his feelings are again divided between an heiress and a courtesan. He chooses a free union with La Nuche, a 'bargain made without the formal foppery of marriage'.

The Lucky Chance shows Behn as a skilled plotter of comedy. It begins with an aggressive preface. Behn claims that her work is underestimated because of her gender:

> Had the Plays I have writ come forth under any Mans Name ...
> I appeal to all unbyast Judges of Sense, if they had not said that
> Person had made as many good Comedies as any one Man that has
> writ in our Age, but a Devil on't the Woman damns the Poet.

Bellmour is in hiding because he has killed a man in a duel. He returns home to discover that it is his beloved Leticia's wedding day. She has married Sir Feeble because the old man tricked her into believing that Bellmour is dead. Leticia agrees not to sleep with her husband. Bellmour disguises himself and ultimately finds out that he has been pardoned for his duel. He claims his rightful bride and the play ends happily. The love triangle in the subplot offers some broader comedy and a more troubling view of marriage. Julia loves Gayman but will not sleep with him 'till the old Gentleman my Husband depart this Wicked World'. Gayman seduces Julia after beating her husband, Sir Cautious, at dice. Instead of paying the debt, Sir Cautious connives in having Gayman smuggled into his wife's bedroom in a chest. Gayman makes love to her in the darkness. In his words, she is an 'innocent Adultress'. Julia is angry but she forgives him when she discovers her husband's part in the trick.

Although the comedy is bawdy, the division between age and youth has an unusual pathos. When Sir Cautious asks Julia if she finds him unattractive, she replies: 'If forty Years were taken from your Age, 'twould render you something more agreeable to my Bed.' When Sir Cautious and Sir Feeble weep together, the audience sympathises. Leticia takes the moral high ground by claiming: 'She cannot from the Paths of Honour rove, / Whose Guide's Religion, and whose End is Love.' But only a fine line divides a combination of religion and love from making a religion of love to justify any betrayal. Gayman is rewarded for his fidelity to Julia with the death of another old man, his uncle, who leaves him 'Two thousand pounds a year'.

Behn's posthumously-staged plays, *The Younger Brother* and *The Widow Ranter*, explore the plight of younger brothers, impoverished by the passing of the family fortune to the eldest son. Neither protagonist sees work as a viable option. George in *The Younger Brother* explains: 'I essay'd to be a plodding Thriver, but found my Parts not form'd for dirty Business.' Hazard in *The Widow Ranter* arrives in Virginia and, when it is suggested that he should find employment, replies, 'I was not born to work, Sir,' and then starts a fight. Both men marry rich women. *The Younger Brother* imitates Wycherley's *The Plain Dealer* but Behn gives a fierce denunciation of arranged and forced marriages when Olivia, declares ''Tis Prostitution in the leudest manner.'

In *The Widow Ranter*, Behn depicts the myths of an emerging nation. The first play to be set in the North American colonies, it reveals a community divided against itself and at war with the Native Americans. The inhabitants of James-Town range from honourable men such as Wellman to dubious characters who have reinvented themselves after fleeing England. Dunce is a self-appointed parson, while Flirt the barmaid implausibly claims, 'My Father was a Baronet.' The play ends with a string of marriages, including that between Daring and the Widow Ranter, a heavy-drinking plain-dealer, who marries while dressed as a man and fights 'like a Fury' at her husband's side. She represents Behn's hope that the new country may have less repressive views on gender than the old.

The tragic plot concerns the love triangle between the Indian King and Queen and the rebellious English general, Bacon. The Queen reveals that she has loved Bacon since she was twelve years old and married the King against her will. Bacon resembles the reckless protagonists of heroic drama. After accidentally killing the disguised Queen, he commits suicide while his soldiers win a battle with both the Native Americans and an army from James-Town. Behn offers an early example of the fated inter-racial relationship, which engages the audience's sympathy but does not unsettle the status quo. The play ends in cautious optimism. Wellman concludes: 'The Governor when he comes, shall find the Country in better hands than he expects to find it.' Summers praised the play as 'photographic in its realism'; even at the last Behn continued to break new artistic ground.

7

William Congreve and the
Melancholic Lunatics

Of the playwrights who began writing in the 1690s, Congreve owes the greatest debt to his elders. His comedies adopt the tropes of the comedy of manners. Dryden and Southerne revised his first play, and his last, *The Way of the World* (1700), is sometimes praised as the 'perfect' Restoration Comedy.

The word 'perfection', with its hint of sterility, is often applied to him. Voltaire comments on his excellence and small output in consecutive sentences: Congreve 'rais'd the Glory of Comedy to a greater Height than any English Writer before or since his Time. He wrote only a few Plays but they are all excellent in their kind.' Voltaire adds: 'The Language is everywhere that of Men of Honour, but their actions are those of Knaves.' Charles Lamb comments in 'On the Artificial Comedy of the Last Century': 'You neither hate nor love his personages.' The cool analysis of his privileged characters entertains but it supposedly does not move an audience. Congreve's plays are more troubling than this discourse of sterile perfectionism suggests.

Congreve's first comedy, *The Old Bachelor* (1693), is efficiently constructed and has no dull stretches but also no originality. It is a competent amalgam of situations from the comedy of manners tradition. Heartwell, is based on Manly in *The Plain Dealer*, as Edmund Gosse notes in his *Life of William Congreve* (1888), and Sophia recalls Olivia from the same play. The pretentious Belinda echoes Melantha from Dryden's *Marriage à la Mode*. The subplot, in which Bellmore seduces Laetitia and is discovered by her husband returning home unexpectedly, is an old standby of farce.

Despite its pervasive borrowings, *The Old Bachelor* impresses with its urban atmosphere. The scenes are often set in London streets and Congreve lets his characters talk on for the pleasure of imitating fashionable conversation. One set piece depicts Heartwell's hesitations before Silvia's home. He despises women but cannot resist her allure:

> **Heartwell:** O thou delicious, damned, dear, destructive woman! 'Sdeath, how the young fellows will hoot me! I shall be the jest of the town. Nay, in two days I expect to be chronicled in ditty, and sung in woeful ballad, to the tune of 'The Superannuated Maiden's Comfort', or 'The Bachelor's Fall'; and upon the third I shall be hanged in effigy, pasted up for the exemplary ornament of necessary-houses and cobblers' stalls. Death, I can't think on't! – I'll run into the danger to lose the apprehension. [*Enters* Silvia's *lodgings.*]

Although *The Old Bachelor* gratifies comic conventions by ending with four weddings, Heartwell remains single. Like Shakespeare's Antonio in *The Merchant of Venice*, his presence introduces doubt into the final celebrations.

Although the play was an immediate success, the high expectations it created for Congreve are surprising. Southerne's poem 'To Mr Congreve, on "The Old Bachelor"', prefaced to the text, asserts that Dryden is the greatest living playwright and Congreve is his successor. Congreve's second play, *The Double Dealer* (1694), was not popular but it impressed Dryden, whose 'To my dear Friend Mr Congreve, on his Comedy called, "The Double Dealer"' claims that Congreve surpasses his rivals at their greatest:

> In him all beauties of this age we see,
> Etherege his courtship, Southerne's purity;
> The satire, wit, and strength of manly Wycherley.

The Double Dealer is more unsettling than *The Old Bachelor*. While the earlier play is largely set outdoors and has a leisurely pace, the action of *The Double Dealer* takes place in a country house over twenty-four hours. With its suggestion of candle-lit interiors, it is literally and metaphorically a darker work. Cynthia and Mellefont are to be married on the following day. The marriage is opposed by Mellefont's stepmother, Lady Touchwood, who tries to seduce him and is already sleeping with his friend Maskwell. Maskwell discredits Mellefont and replaces him as the heir to the Touchwood estate. He also attempts to marry Cynthia. The deception is revealed when Cynthia and Lord Touchwood hide behind a screen and overhear Maskwell and Lady Touchwood discuss their affair. Mellefont is restored to his father's favour and the play ends with his approaching wedding.

Touchwood's discovery of his wife's infidelity makes him the most tragic of three cuckolded husbands. In the two subplots, the pretentiously intellectual Lady Froth and the fashionable Lady Plyant take lovers. If Touchwood's marital unhappiness darkens the conclusion, the other intrigues offer a compensating lightness of touch. Lady Plyant accepts Careless' proposition while seeming to refuse it: 'I could resist the strongest temptation. – But yet I know, 'tis impossible for me to know whether I could or not; there's no certainty in the things of this life.'

Congreve defended his play against critics who disliked Maskwell's soliloquies: 'No other better way [has] yet [been] invented for the communication of thought.' These soliloquies offer an analysis of man's inevitable dishonesty to man:

> Ha! but is there not such a thing as honesty? Yes, and whosoever has it about him bears an enemy in his breast: for your honest man, as I take it, is that nice scrupulous conscientious person, who will cheat nobody but himself.

Congreve expands on this bleak view of society in his *Amendments of Mr Collier's False and Imperfect Citations*, his defence of the comedy of manners against Collier's charges of immorality. Congreve asks where a gloomier people may be found than the English:

> Are we not of all people the most unfit to be alone, and most unsafe to be trusted ourselves? Are there not more self-murderers and melancholic lunatics in England, heard of in one year, than in a great part of Europe besides?

The theatre offers a defence against this suicidal melancholia. This depressive vision pervades *The Double Dealer* and Congreve's subsequent plays. Maskwell's soliloquies suggest that he does not so much plot evil schemes as watch his own mind unfold those schemes. Gosse complains that Maskwell 'is a devil, pure and simple, and not a man at all'. But Gosse underestimates the human capacity for hypocrisy. More plausibly, he suggests that the play resembles *Tartuffe*. Like Maskwell, Molière's Tartuffe becomes the trusted guest in a prosperous household. Both men plot to seduce the wife, discredit the son and receive his inheritance. Both are exposed when the concealed husband overhears a compromising discussion. In *Tartuffe*, the faithful wife stages the conversation to reveal Tartuffe's hypocrisy but in *The Double Dealer* Lady Touchwood is unaware of her husband's presence.

Love for Love (1695) was a popular success and, after the experimental *The Double Dealer*, a return to safer ground. Valentine is impoverished by his own recklessness and the ill will of his father, Sir Sampson. The play opens with Valentine reading Epictetus and ironically praising poverty in a scene that recalls the beginning of Shadwell's *The Virtuoso*, where Bruce reads Lucretius. Valentine loves Angelica, but his chances of marrying her are reduced by his father's determination to make a younger son, the sailor Ben, his heir and marry him to 'a silly awkward country Girl'. Prue is not the only stock type in the play. Mrs Frail is a promiscuous society lady who values her respectability. The occultist Foresight is probably inspired by the pseudo-scientist, Sir Nicholas Gimcrack, in *The Virtuoso*. Both men are cuckolds who spout absurd theories. Ben provides some entertaining nautical dialogue which becomes funnier when Mrs Frail, hearing of Ben's inheritance, uses the same vocabulary to court him.

Valentine pretends to be mad to avoid signing a document transferring his inheritance to Ben. Although Angelica is not convinced by his performance, she realises that it is Valentine she loves. His eventual decision to sign the document rather than lose any hope of marrying her is a test of character. He keeps his fortune and wins Angelica. Sir Sampson is mocked for his hard-heartedness and Ben returns to sea. The beau Tattle and Mrs Frail are tricked into marrying each other by the witty servant Jeremy.

Love for Love is Congreve's most cheerful and most stageworthy comedy, offering numerous set pieces: including Valentine's madness, Ben's inept courtship of Prue, Foresight's mystical ramblings and Mrs Frail's seduction of Ben. But Congreve's melancholy shows through the humour. Valentine has several illegitimate children, mentioned in Act I. They will probably benefit from his restored wealth but will he be a more loving father than Sir Sampson? Remarkably, when Ben asks after a third son, Sir Sampson replies: 'Dick has been dead these two years!' Ben admits that he received the news but 'had forgot'. Valentine and Ben address each other only once. The Legend family is united by financial ties alone.

The Mourning Bride (1697) was Congreve's most popular play during his lifetime. Samuel Johnson praises one passage as the finest speech ever written in English but the play's reputation declined in the nineteenth century. Gosse claims that 'It has been the habit to quote *The Mourning Bride* as the very type of bad declamatory tragedy.' As with *The Old Bachelor*, Congreve combines the most popular elements of his chosen genre: *The Mourning Bride* is set in Spain during the conflict between Christians and Moors; the hero is loved by his devoted, high-minded wife and a royal temptress. During the incongruous final scene, marital love triumphs among a welter of violent deaths. All these traits are found in Dryden's *The Conquest of Granada* or Lee's *The Rival Queens*, while the confusions caused by a headless corpse dressed in another man's clothes derive from Shakespeare's *Cymbeline*.

Congreve's show-stopper comes in Act II. Almeria, the daughter of the King of Granada, has secretly married Alphonso, the son of her father's dead enemy, King Anselmo. Alphonso has supposedly died in battle and his wife visits Anselmo's tomb at night to mourn. In her misery she calls his name and Alphonso emerges from his father's tomb. In its use of darkness, mystery, a setting designed to inspire awe, and the appearance of a (seemingly) ghostly figure, this scene is a precursor of the Gothic literature that became popular later in the eighteenth century. It can also be read as a metaphor of depression: the hero, lost among the dead, is called back to life by the voice of the woman he loves.

The Way of the World (1700) has a paradoxical reputation. It is praised as Congreve's masterpiece and yet regarded as 'too perfect' for performance. In his novel, *Next Season* (1969), Michael Blakemore's actor-director, Ivan Spears, argues that the play is 'flawed by its own excellence, mothered out of existence by an oversolicitous author. The plot is so refined and complicated, so devious, that in performance the play seems to have no story at all.' Gosse is equally ambivalent. His assessment is that '*The Way of the World* is the best-written, the most intellectually accomplished of all English comedies, perhaps of all the comedies of the world.' It disappoints however on the stage: 'The spectator fidgets in his stall, and wishes that the actors and actresses would be doing something.'

It is difficult to account for this play's reputation for complexity. The only confusion in *The Way of the World* derives from trying to decide how the hero, Mirabell, is superior to the villain Fainall. Both men are schemers in search of a fortune. Previously Mirabell, fearing that his mistress may be pregnant, has tricked Fainall into marrying her; Mirabell explains: 'A better man ought not to have been sacrificed to the occasion; a worse had not answered to the purpose.' Fainall loves Mrs Marwood but he depends on his wife's money. He has been placed by Mirabell in a comfortable hell in which he clearly sees the hypocrisy of everyone, including his mistress:

Fainall: O the pious friendships of the female sex!
Mrs Marwood: More tender, more sincere, and more enduring, than all the vain and empty vows of men, whether professing love to us, or mutual faith to one another.
Fainall: Ha, ha, ha; you are my wife's friend too.

In contrast to the impulsive Valentine of *Love for Love*, Mirabell is a calculating character. Valentine's madness hardly fools anyone but Mirabell's schemes are carefully planned. His attempt to humiliate Lady Wishfort by having his disguised servant go through a mock wedding with her fails only because Mrs Marwood reveals the plot. Mirabell immediately initiates a second, successful plan to gain the Lady's consent to his marriage with Millamant. Congreve begins his play with a card game and ends with a battle of wits. His point is not the moral one that 'Good shall prevail' but the capitalist one that success is everything.

Despite its serious themes, *The Way of the World* gives an impression of light-heartedness. Although set in London, it reveals Congreve's love of the Irish tall story. Lady Wishfort's account of her daughter's purity anticipates the rambling, absurdist tone of Samuel Beckett's monologues:

I chiefly made it my own care to initiate her very infancy in the rudiments of virtue, and to impress upon her tender years a young odium and aversion to the very sight of men:–ay, friend, she would ha' shrieked if she had but seen a man, till she was in her teens. As I am a person 'tis true;– she was never suffered to play with a male child, though but in coats; nay, her very babies were of the feminine gender. Oh, she never looked a man in the face but her own father, or the chaplain, and him we made a shift to put upon her for a woman, by the help of his long garments, and his sleek face, till she was going in her fifteen.

The comparative failure of the first production of *The Way of the World* has been blamed for Congreve's subsequent silence as a playwright. Collier's moralising criticism and Dryden's death perhaps contributed but Congreve's silence resulted from a prolonged depression caused by his own moral vision. He confessed to John Dennis: 'I could never look long upon a monkey without very mortifying reflections.' After 1700, he continued to be involved with the theatre for another decade. He co-managed the Drury Lane Theatre and encouraged a new generation of playwrights including Catherine Trotter and Mary Pix. His last work for the stage was an opera libretto, *Semele* (1707), which considers the limits of human happiness:

> Mortals whom Gods affect
> Have narrow Limits set to Life,
> And cannot long be bless'd.

The composer for whom Congreve wrote the text was John Eccles, the Master of the Queen's Musick, but the work was not performed at the time, perhaps because of its licentious plot and the growing public preference for Italian opera. Handel, however, turned to Congreve's libretto for his very operatic oratorio of 1743, and though he had no great success with it at the time, in recent decades *Semele* has become one of his best-known operas – and consequently perhaps the most frequently performed of Congreve's stage works.

8

'This Adultery of the Mind': The Second Generation

In 1688, the Catholic King James II was forced to abandon the throne of England, and at the start of 1689 was succeeded jointly by his Protestant daughter Mary and her Dutch husband, William, Prince of Orange. During this 'Glorious Revolution', political oaths and family ties were betrayed and Members of Parliament helped William's foreign army to invade England. The new regime claimed legitimacy on the grounds that it would ensure England remained Protestant. In contrast to the sexual promiscuity that had marked the court of Charles II, William and Mary promoted respectability and domestic harmony. The theatre reflected the new tone of the court. Marriage had become the safeguard of national morality. The question the plays asked was: what made a good marriage?

The playwrights of the 1690s were an increasingly diverse group. They brought new perspectives to the conventions of Restoration drama. Thomas Southerne and George Farquhar had Irish backgrounds. They began the emigration of talent which made Kenneth Tynan pronounce (in *The Observer,* 21st November 1954) that 'English drama is a procession of glittering Irishmen' (later to include Richard Brinsley Sheridan, Oscar Wilde and George Bernard Shaw). John Vanbrugh's family had escaped religious persecution in Holland in the previous century and made their money in the sugar industry. Following Aphra Behn, more women, including Susannah Centlivre and Mary Pix, began to write for the public stage.

Southerne has been criticised as a populist playwright. The editor of the 1774 edition of his works, Thomas Evans, admits: 'Southerne was a slave to custom; he saw and lamented the taste of the times, but knew, to ensure success, that taste must be followed.' Consequently, he is a useful indicator of changing fashions. His best work was written during the 1690s. He began the decade with a bawdy comedy and ended it as a master of emotionally-charged high drama. He became a favourite author among women, writing sympathetically about their social condition, and was valued for his command of pathos.

In *Sir Antony Love* (1690), three young Englishmen in France court women and joke about standard Restoration subjects: sex, money and the falsity of social conventions. The play mocks Catholicism: a pilgrim proves to be a confidence man and a likeable Abbé is secretly homosexual. Despite their fast talk, Southerne's heroes and heroines remain chaste. Valentine and Foriante marry for love; Charlotte marries a Count for his title and to avoid becoming a nun, and Volante accepts a dependable man after a romantic disappointment. Sir Antony (Lydia in disguise) tricks Sir Giles, her seducer, into marriage and then agrees to a separation for a large financial settlement.

Sir Antony is a 'breeches part' (played by a woman). These roles depend on the theatrical convention that the other characters are taken in by the disguise but the audience can enjoy the view of the actress' feminine curves made possible by her masculine clothing. Southerne provides more conventional breeches parts in *The Fatal Marriage* (1694) and *Oroonoko* (1695) but Sir Antony transcends gender. Society women love 'his' sympathy, men envy 'his' wit, the Abbé desires 'him' and the less than fastidious Pilgrim suspects the truth but confesses: 'I am resolv'd to like you in any sex.'

The opening scene of *The Wives' Excuse* (1691) reveals a different kind of uncertainty, that of class. Footmen gossip while waiting for their employers at a Music Evening. They boast that they sometimes father their masters' supposed children. Two pages, imitating the conversation of society women, imply that if French soldiers invaded England these women would enjoy being 'ravished'. For Southerne, the barriers between classes were becoming negotiable. A servant might even see his illegitimate son, born to his employer's wife, inherit a fortune.

In the main plot, Lovemore and Mrs Witwoud conspire to disillusion Mrs Friendall with her superficial husband so that Lovemore may seduce her. They incite Ruffle to strike Friendall. This is meant to provoke a duel but Mrs Friendall intervenes. She fears that her husband is a coward and asks: 'Can I love the man I most despise?' Lovemore escorts her to St James' Park, where Friendall solicits his own masked wife, taking her to be a prostitute. As a man of fashion, he thinks it his part to enjoy the favours of other women.

As his name suggests, he courts universal approval and pays for it with expensive wines, tea and tobacco.

Mrs Friendall, surprisingly, refuses to seek revenge against her husband by becoming an adulteress. She will not compromise her self-worth and tells the disappointed Lovemore that 'What I do is for my own sake.' She knows, however, that women are the greater victims in unhappy marriages, which 'condemn us to a slavery of life'. Southerne returns repeatedly to the theme of marriage as the enslavement of wives.

Brean Hammon called Southerne 'the Restoration Chekhov'. Like Chekhov, he depicts life-sapping relationships with subtlety but the comparison should be treated with caution; where Chekhov innovates, Southerne works in the conventions of his time, manipulating them to his own purposes. In a common Restoration device, Friendall and Mrs Witwoud have sex, both masked, and each mistaking the other's identity. At the same time Southerne emphasises the theatricality of his work: Wellville intends to write a play called *The Wives' Excuse* – the title of the play he is acting in.

In *The Fatal Marriage; or, The Innocent Adultery* (1694), Villeroy has courted the impoverished widow Isabella for seven years. He is encouraged by her villainous brother-in-law Carlos. Isabella begs her father-in-law, Count Baldwin, for money to feed her son. Baldwin blames her for his son Biron's death at the siege of Candy and refuses. Her debts are paid by Villeroy and Isabella feels obliged to marry him. Biron turns out to have been enslaved but not killed. He returns and is rescued by Villeroy from an attack by Carlos' hired thugs. Isabella is confronted by her two husbands before Biron dies from his wounds. Carlos had suppressed Biron's letters and deliberately encouraged Isabella's bigamous remarriage. Isabella stabs herself, commending her son to Villeroy and the repentant Baldwin before dying.

The Fatal Marriage, like Aphra Behn's last plays, criticises the widespread practice of primogeniture, designed to keep great estates intact by bequest of the inheritance to the eldest son alone, leaving younger sons and unmarried daughters with a pittance. Carlos insists that he would not have tried to supplant his elder brother if he had been treated with kindness by his father and promised some financial security.

Isabella's bigamy follows the tradition of plays about 'innocent adulteries', including Otway's *The Orphan* and Dryden's *Amphitryon*. Isabella had intended to be a nun before meeting Biron. Forgiven by the Church, she still fears God's anger. Balanced against Southerne's progressive view of parental responsibility is a bleaker morality demanding the punishment of transgression. Isabella has been unfaithful to God, and God, by compelling her infidelity to Biron, becomes another cruel father.

Oroonoko, like *The Fatal Marriage*, is based on a story by Aphra Behn. In his dedication, Southerne ponders why Behn did not dramatise her novel: 'She thought either that no actor could represent him, or she could not bear him represented.' Oroonoko has the passionate impulsiveness which defines the protagonists of heroic dramas. In a comic subplot, Welldon (Charlotte disguised as a man) and her sister Lucy have left London for Surinam to find husbands among the slave-holders. This subplot complements the main theme: the hero's literal slavery is analogous to the metaphorical slavery of women in marriage. But Southerne does not see slavery as necessarily immoral. Oroonoko sells slaves before he is betrayed. Slavery in this play is evil when it leads to sexual exploitation. The Widow Lackitt laments that she cannot father slaves as her male rivals do. Blanford refuses to sell Imoinda to the Lieutenant Governor because he fears that she would be raped. Unlike Behn's 'black Venus', Southerne's Imoinda is white. Slavery becomes a social issue as much as a racial one. The satire is directed against unscrupulous parvenus like Captain Driver. Old money is supposedly guided by a framework of benign custom but new money is lawless and lacks virtue.

It is not the noble Oroonoko who initiates the slaves' rebellion but his servant Aboan. There is a parallel with Shakespeare's *Julius Caesar*. Oroonoko, like Brutus, makes idealistic decisions which doom the revolt to failure. He stops Aboan from murdering Hoffman, who warns the slave-holders of the uprising. Aboan rightly sees that Blanford cannot protect the slaves from Driver, the Lieutenant Governor of the corrupt slave-holding community. As Jack Stanmore argues, their demand for Oroonoko's execution has nothing to do with justice: 'Guilty or not is not the business. Hanging is their sport.'

In 1696, the young actor Colley Cibber wrote *Love's Last Shift*. His dedication gratefully mentions Southerne's support. Cibber creates a main plot in which Amanda forgives her estranged husband his infidelities. She disguises herself as a prostitute to seduce Loveless back into matrimonial virtue. The play ends with the couple reunited. Cibber's combination of four acts of titillation with a fifth act of repentance proved popular but Vanbrugh was unimpressed. *The*

Relapse is a sequel to *Love's Last Shift*, which questions many of Cibber's assumptions about marriage and morality. Vanbrugh borrows his plot from *The Wives' Excuse*. His Amanda is also the victim of a conspiracy to destroy her marriage. Berinthia seduces Loveless while Worthy tries to use this betrayal to persuade Amanda to accept his advances. Like Mrs Friendall, Amanda refuses out of self-respect.

Dobrée claims that Vanbrugh's moral vision undermines his comic intentions: 'The persons of his plays commit adultery with the full knowledge that they are acting contrary to their own morality,' and this creates 'an atmosphere of lasciviousness which destroys the comic'. This judgement does not take account of the broad humour of the scenes involving Lord Foppington, and Young Fashion's journey to Sir Tunbelly's country home. Much of Vanbrugh's comedy however subtly permeates the decisions made by Loveless and Amanda.

Loveless' lukewarm praise of 'lawful love' in his opening monologue conveys his desire for the alternative:

The raging flame of wild destructive lust,
Reduced to a warm pleasing fire of lawful love,
My life glides on, and all is well within.

The joke is on Loveless' capacity for self-delusion but it also questions the ideal of the 'happy marriage'. Amanda has become known in London society for forgiving her ruined husband after ten years of estrangement; Vanbrugh examines the psychological cost of such conspicuous virtue. In Cibber's play, Amanda declares: 'All the comfort of my Life is, that I can tell my Conscience, I have been true to Virtue.' Vanbrugh's Amanda, however, is curious about the pleasure she refuses, and questions both Foppington and Berinthia about their love affairs.

The overall impact of *The Relapse* suggests variety rather than pathos. The supporting cast threatens to upstage the protagonists. The homosexual marriage broker, Coupler, is irrepressible in his advances to young men; Foppington is an unfailing delight. Through his affected pronunciation, his father's fatal accident becomes a surreal bowel movement: he was 'shat through the head'. Sir Tunbelly Clumsy and Hoyden introduce an anarchic energy and their country home offers a wide range of directorial possibilities: it can be an idyllic rural retreat, a bleak, rain-soaked ruin or both in different scenes. The political divide is pervasive. Foppington has bought his peerage from the new regime though his brother stays loyal to James II. Sir Tunbelly asks him: 'Are you a Williamite, or a Jacobite?' The play evokes a world of new men, new ways and new loyalties.

Vanbrugh's approach becomes more schematic after *The Relapse*. His other plays gain the sharper edges of moral fables but lose a degree of emotional complexity. *The Provoked Wife* (1697) begins like a university debate; Sir John Brute speaks a monologue about the unhappiness of married men, and his wife retorts with a speech about the sorrow of married women. He stays with her only through cowardice: 'Would my courage come up but to a fourth part of my ill nature, I'd stand buff to her relations, and thrust her out of doors.' Like Squire Sullen in Farquhar's *The Beaux' Stratagem* (1707), Sir John is a melancholy ruffian. His heavy drinking is driven by self-loathing. Lord Rake's song is to his 'taste' because it celebrates pleasure without guilt:

> No saucy remorse
> Intrudes in my course,
> Nor impertinent notions of evil.
> So there's claret in store,
> In peace I've my whore,
> And in peace I jog on to the devil.

Unfortunately 'impertinent notions of evil' frequently disturb the protagonists. Lady Brute agrees to deceive her husband but is prevented by chance and feels 'saucy remorse'. Lady Fancyfull, the female fop, faces a moral confrontation when Heartfree arranges to meet her in St James' Park. Given the park's reputation, she expects an affair, but Heartfree is out to destroy her vanity:

> **Heartfree:** You are the most ungrateful woman upon earth.
> **Lady Fancyfull:** Ungrateful! To who?
> **Heartfree:** To nature.
> **Lady Fancyfull:** Why, what has nature done for me?
> **Heartfree:** What you have undone by art. It made you handsome, it gave you beauty to a miracle, a shape without a fault, wit enough to make 'em relish, and so turned you loose to your own discretion; which has made such work with you, that you are become the pity of our sex, and the jest of your own. There is not a feature in your face, but you have found the way to teach it some affected convulsion.

Though she denies the charges, Lady Fancyfull finds Heartfree more attractive after this encounter. She attempts to discredit her rival, Belinda, and is humiliated. Like Lord Foppington, she amuses because she is so truly in love with herself but she is trapped in her role and cannot imagine a life outside it. Her revenge is that she steals all her scenes. She has the best lines and draws the eye with her outlandish costumes. Micheál MacLiammóir recalls, in *All for Hecuba* (1946), that he designed an extravagant costume for her so that she looked 'like a fantastically expensive gilt cracker'.

The Confederacy (1705) and the unfinished *A Journey to London* (1728) depict a society in which men and women are radically divided from each other. These plays also address an increasing unease about the dangers of gambling. It was feared that women who had lost all their money would pay their debts by prostituting themselves to their creditors. In *The Confederacy*, Gripe and Moneytrap, two rich citizens, want to sleep with each other's wives. Clarissa and Araminta realise this and extort money out of their husbands to set up a Basset table (essentially a gambling syndicate) while remaining chaste. The play suggests that when women form a 'confederacy' they can easily outwit men. The best scene involves an argument between Gripe and Clarissa. She concedes every point to her husband but gets exactly what she wants. A secondary theme is social climbing. The working-class Dick Amlet masquerades as Colonel Shapely to marry well. In a final twist, his mother is revealed to be the richest character in the play, having amassed a fortune by selling cosmetics, false teeth and even wooden legs to society women.

Brean Hammond, in his introduction to *The Relapse and Other Plays* (2004), finds *A Journey to London* 'heavy-handedly patriarchal'. It is tempting to see the modest Clarinda as a golden mean between Loverule's unimaginative routine and Lady Arabella's pursuit of excitement in gambling (and one which would be applauded by the men in the audience) but Vanbrugh challenges Clarinda's 'sober' code even as he states it. To 'go to a masquerade soberly' betrays the experience; a masquerade should involve a spirit of mystery and adventure, otherwise there is no point in going. Her philosophy is prudent but limiting. Arabella is at her worst when she refuses to pay her debt to Shortyard so that she can gamble the money away; but she recognises that life has more to offer than obedience to her tepid husband's rules. Vanbrugh anticipates William Blake's aphorism that 'The road of excess leads to the palace of wisdom.'

Like Vanbrugh, George Farquhar explores the tension between constraint and liberty. Farquhar studied at Trinity College, Dublin and acted at the Smock Alley Theatre. He soon followed Robert Wilks, who acted the protagonists in his plays, to London; the two men formed an important creative friendship. Farquhar's plays fall into three groups. *Love in a Bottle* (1698) and *The Constant Couple* (1699) adopt the conventions of Restoration comedy. After the spectacular success of *The Constant Couple*, the twenty-one-year-old playwright floundered in his middle period. The disappointing sequel, *Sir Harry Wildair* (1701) contributes to the 'gaming play' genre by depicting Lady Lurewell as a gambler. He adapted Beaumont and Fletcher's *The Wild Goose Chase* (1621?) as *The Inconstant* (1702) and wrote the experimental *The Twin Rivals* (1702). His commission as a recruiting officer took him to Shrewsbury and Lichfield. These small cities inspired his best plays, *The Recruiting Officer* (1706) and *The Beaux' Stratagem*. He died before his thirtieth birthday.

Wycherley and Congreve had celebrated wit. Farquhar's ideal was 'good humour' or 'good nature', a generous and forgiving trait. While wit reduces life to a neat epigram, humour deals in exaggeration. Both Farquhar and Susanna Centlivre employ what Thalia Stathas calls 'tolerant laughter', by which vice and hypocrisy are revealed but the culprits are not humiliated. *The Constant Couple* is a transitional work. It contains Restoration stereotypes such as the heiress, the pious hypocrite and the vengeful woman. Lady Lurewell's family name is Manly, recalling Wycherley's hero in *The Plain Dealer*. Like her namesake, she takes a cruel pleasure in exposing hypocrisy. Seduced as a young woman, she seeks revenge against all men. Her foil is Sir Harry Wildair, a free spirit incapable of hypocrisy. Wildair shakes off the restraints of Restoration comedy. He is not often witty but his humour is vigorous and mordant; Lady Lurewell asks him about mutual acquaintances in Paris:

> **Lady Lurewell:** And where my Count Le Valier?
> **Wildair:** His body's in the church of Nôtre Dame; I don't know where his soul is.
> **Lady Lurewell:** What disease did he die of?
> **Wildair:** A duel, madam; I was his doctor.
> **Lady Lurewell:** How d'ye mean?
> **Wildair:** As most doctors do, I killed him!

Vizard tells Wildair that Angelica is an expensive prostitute; she believes he has come to present himself as a potential husband and is outraged when he makes increasingly offensive advances. In the 1740s Wildair became a breeches part, perhaps because his swaggering masculinity verges on parody.

The humour in *The Constant Couple* anticipates absurdist theatre in its playfulness and use of phrases drained of meaning. The constable's interrogation of Clincher Senior mocks an inarticulate aristocracy.

> **Constable:** How came you by these clothes, sir?
> **Clincher Senior:** You must know, sir, that walking along, sir, I don't know how, sir, I can't tell where, sir; and – so the porter and I changed clothes, sir.
> **Constable:** Very well. The man speaks reason and like a gentleman.

In the preface to *The Twin Rivals*, Farquhar complains that his audience will not accept a play without Restoration comedy stereotypes:

> They take all innovations for grievances … A play without a beau, cully, cuckold, or coquette, is as poor an entertainment to some palates, as their Sunday's dinner would be without beef and pudding.

The Twin Rivals follows the parallel attempts of two villains to accomplish their schemes. Richmore is a wealthy seducer who enjoys ruining women's reputations. He has made Clelia (who never appears onstage) pregnant but refuses to marry her. Instead he pursues Aurelia, loved by the 'good-natured' Trueman. After assaulting Aurelia, Richmore is defeated in combat by Trueman, repents and marries Clelia. The hunchback Benjamin fakes his elder twin's death to inherit an estate and tries to seduce Constance. Hermes, with the help of his servant Teague, outwits Benjamin and regains his property and his bride. Teague provides comic relief with his overblown Irish accent, especially when he recalls Carrickfergus, his home 'shitty'.

The two plots are united by the midwife Mrs Mandrake, who pimps for Richmore and perjures herself by swearing that Benjamin was born before Hermes. She assists pregnant society women, including Clelia and the ominously named Lady Stillborn. Farquhar depicts a side of the libertine lifestyle that his predecessors ignored: the money made from unwanted babies and secret abortions.

After *The Twin Rivals*, Farquhar incorporated some conventional elements into his last plays to reassure his audience. *The Recruiting Officer* and *The Beaux' Stratagem* provide gallant heroes who balance their finer feelings for heiresses with their unprincipled seduction of lower-class girls. But Farquhar introduces unorthodox touches. During both plays the offstage death of a brother has important consequences. Owen's death in *The Recruiting Officer* turns Sylvia into an heiress, so that her father no longer regards Plume as a good match. At the end of *The Beaux' Stratagem*, the news of the death of Aimwell's elder brother is received with joy. Shakespeare had ended a comedy with an offstage death in *Love's Labour's Lost* but with Farquhar any grief takes second place to questions of inheritance.

Farquhar broke away from the London-based model of Restoration comedy. In *Letters to George* (1989), Max Stafford-Clark claims:

> *The Recruiting Officer* represents a major departure in realism for it is the first major English play that gives a serious picture of country life and not an assemblage of rustic eccentrics designed to titillate the metropolitan palate. In most Restoration drama the country is equated with stifling stupidity.

Farquhar's focus on small communities is important. If Plume had fathered an illegitimate child in London the matter would hardly have been noticed but in Shrewsbury everyone knows about Molly's disgrace. As Worthy says: 'There have been tears in town about that business.' Sylvia's decision to support the baby may be a charitable action but it is also a public declaration of ownership and indirectly asserts her claim to Plume. Equally, from Harriet in *The Man of Mode* to Hoyden in *The Relapse*, women with social or intellectual aspirations long to escape from the country to London. But the emphasis changes in *The Beaux' Stratagem*. Mrs Sullen is unhappily married and this alone determines her dislike of Lichfield.

The Recruiting Officer is Farquhar's most original play. Shakespeare portrays the cynicism of recruitment in *Henry IV, Part One*, and Otway shows disillusioned soldiers coming home in *The Soldier's Fortune*. But Farquhar was the first dramatist to celebrate the theatricality of the army, not in war but in its everyday activities. He begins *The Recruiting Officer* with a sound cue, the beating of the regimental drum. Then Kite gives his recruiting speech, which resembles reportage, except that his promises of adventure, social status and wealth are laced with irony: 'This is the cap of honour, it dubs a man a gentleman in the drawing of a trigger.' Kite is not lying but he says nothing of the perils of army life. (Farquhar's *Love and a Bottle* begins with Roebuck meeting a cripple 'five years a soldier, and fifteen years a beggar'. The hero concludes that 'the merciful bullet' would have been a kinder end to the man's life.)

Because of this cynicism, twentieth-century dramatists often saw a subversive message in Farquhar's play. Bertolt Brecht adapted it as *Trumpets and Drums* (1955); it influenced John Arden's pacifist *Serjeant Musgrave's Dance* (1959); and Timberlake Wertenbaker's *Our Country's Good* (1988), based around the performance of *The Recruiting Officer* (the first play performed in Australia) by convicts in 1789, emphasises the play's class and gender divisions. But *The Recruiting Officer* was popular with Farquhar's fellow officers. Arguably, it suggests that army life is more honest than civilian life. Although the military corruption is blatant, the soldiers openly acknowledge that their trade is war, while civilians wage an undeclared war for profit and power.

In this clandestine war, Sylvia is a strategic genius who outwits her father, Melinda and Plume. Melinda points out Sylvia's 'masculine' mentality: 'Hadst thou been a man, thou hadst been the greatest rake in Christendom.' Melinda is conducting her own war against Worthy. Previously Worthy had offered her a yearly allowance to become his mistress. She asked for a week to consider the proposition and suddenly inherited a fortune. By not immediately rejecting his proposal, it is implied that she would probably have agreed. Her reunion with Worthy is nuanced by the tension between their mutual attraction, her anger at his proposition and disgust with herself at having even thought about acceptance.

Farquhar brings a new profundity to Restoration stereotypes. Although Balance plays the traditional role of the 'blocking' father, he values Sylvia's opinions and wants to protect her. Their conversations anticipate those of Mr Bennet with Elizabeth in Jane Austen's *Pride and Prejudice* (1813). Balance is devastatingly honest on hearing of his son's illness: 'I was pleased with the death of my father, because he left me an estate, and now I'm punished with the loss of an heir to inherit mine.' Equally, Kite is a witty servant: cunning, prone to outlandish disguises (his performance as a fortune teller) and endowed with an eye for the main chance. But he shows self-awareness in his summary of his career:

I was born a gipsy, and bred among that crew till I was ten year old. There I learned canting and lying. I was bought from my mother, Cleopatra, by a certain nobleman for three pistols; who, liking my beauty, made me his page; there I learned impudence and pimping. I was turned off for wearing my lord's linen, and drinking my lady's ratafia, and then turned bailiff's follower: there I learned bullying and swearing. I at last got into the army, and there I learned whoring and drinking: so that if your worship pleases to cast up the whole sum, viz., canting, lying, impudence, pimping, bullying, swearing, whoring, drinking, and a halberd, you will find the sum total will amount to a recruiting serjeant.

Stafford-Clark describes this monologue as 'a picture of a brutalised psychopath'. It could equally well be taken as the frank self-portrait of a man who is determined to survive and turn any situation to his advantage.

The Beaux' Stratagem is also about survival. Archer and Aimwell have pooled their dwindling resources. Their stratagem involves travelling in search of heiresses with the agreement that whoever marries first will subsidise his friend. They alternate the roles of master and servant in each new town to give the illusion of wealth. If their trick is unsuccessful and their money runs out, they will enlist to fight in the War of the Spanish Succession. Consequently, the comedy has a background of potential mortality. Archer boasts: 'We may die, as we lived, in a blaze.'

Farquhar does not depict his protagonists as outright villains like Richmore and Benjamin in *The Twin Rivals*. Aimwell falls in love with Dorinda and ultimately refuses to trick her into marriage. On hearing of his elder brother's death, he discovers that he has become the lord he pretends to be. Archer is more of a realist: 'There is no scandal like rags, nor any crime so shameful as poverty.' His attempted seduction of Mrs Sullen becomes a courageous rescue when Lady Bountiful's home is burgled. But he unrepentantly continues his courtship: 'I'm none of your romantic fools, that fight giants and monsters for nothing.'

William Hazlitt judges, in *Lectures on the English Comic Writers* (1819), that Archer and Aimwell 'are real gentlemen, and only pretended imposters'. Ann Blake's introduction to the New Mermaid edition (2006) of the play adds that to 'argue that Farquhar is presenting serious social criticism here is a mistake. Comic values prevail; the beaux's stratagem is quarantined from criticism.' But *The*

Beaux' Stratagem expresses serious social criticism by depicting the vulnerability of Lady Bountiful's home. The house is subject to three attacks: burglary by Gibbet's gang, Archer's attempted seduction of Mrs Sullen and Aimwell's fraudulent courtship of Dorinda. It is also weakened by internal divisions. The Sullens hate each other, while Lady Bountiful, who represents the social apex of the play, becomes absurd when she inadvertently suggests that the medicine she inflicts on the peasantry is her own urine: 'You shall taste my water; 'tis a cordial I can assure, and of my own making – '

Archer's relationship with Cherry also questions class assumptions. Just as Plume woos Rose, 'a Country Wench' in *The Recruiting Officer*, Archer flirts with the innkeeper's daughter. Both men think of bedding a lower-class girl as a pleasant distraction from the serious business of courting an heiress. Rose is predictably gullible, but Cherry has more depth. Archer mocks her gentility: 'She reads plays, keeps a monkey, and is troubled with vapours.' Farquhar, however, gives poignancy to her outburst: 'Though I was born to servitude, I hate it.' Eventually, Archer confides in her and she proposes marriage, a notably independent gesture in a time when women were expected to wait for a man to make the offer:

> **Archer:** … I was born a gentleman, my education was liberal; but I went to London, a younger brother, fell into the hands of sharpers, who stripped me of my money, my friends disowned me, and now my necessity brings me to what you see.
> **Cherry:** Then take my hand – promise to marry me before you sleep, and I'll make you master of two thousand pounds.

Archer snobbishly refuses: 'an innkeeper's daughter; ay, that's the devil – ' After Cherry reveals the scheme to rob Lady Bountiful's home, he asks for her to be appointed Dorinda's maid – a poor reward but it gives Cherry contact with a grand family and brings her closer to achieving her ambitions.

The play is noted for its advocacy of divorce. The references to unhappy marriages range from Gibbet the highwayman's small courtesy to one of his victims ('She told me of her husband's barbarous usage, and so I left her half-a-Crown.') to Dorinda's warning against provoking Sullen's jealousy: 'Who knows how far his brutality may carry him?' The Sullens are both sardonic about their marriage. Mrs Sullen exclaims: 'Oh, the pleasure of counting the melancholy clock by a snoring husband!' Not recognising his own brother-in-law, Sir Charles Freeman, Sullen offers to pass on his wife: 'You shall have her to-morrow morning, and a venison-pasty into the bargain.' Their eventual separation is ambivalent. Ann Blake notes that 'Only six divorces were granted in the years between 1660 and 1714.' She regards 'the liberation of Mrs Sullen' as 'legally impossible', but Sir Charles' claim that 'Consent is law enough to set you free' carries theatrical if not legal authority. Farquhar's realism is not shown in this 'happy' divorce but in the questions it raises about Dorinda's naïve expectations of marriage: 'If I marry my Lord Aimwell, there will be title, place, and precedence, the Park, the play, and the drawing-room, splendour, equipage, noise, and flambeaux.'

Susanna Centlivre's early comedies, *The Gamester* and *The Basset Table* (both 1705), are 'gaming plays' and contribute to the debate on marriage. Such plays suggest that women have pleasures greater than their relationships with men. In Cibber's *The Provoked Husband* (1728), an adaptation of Vanbrugh's *A Journey to London*, Lord Townly calls his wife's passion for all-night gambling 'this adultery of the mind'. The gaming Lady Reveller in *The Basset Table* refuses to remarry. Sir James Courtly's successful scheme to scare her into Lord Worthy's arms with a threatened rape suggests the vulnerability even of titled women.

Centlivre was a prolific professional playwright. Although her politics were opposed to Aphra Behn's, she encountered similar prejudices. Centlivre suffered particularly from accusations of plagiarism. Her preface to *Love's Contrivance* (1703) argues of the adaptation of French plays: 'Who e'er borrows from them, must take care to touch the colours with an English pencil, and form the Piece according to our Manners.' She may have recalled Wycherley's example and she often borrows from him. The subplot of *The Busy Body* (1709), in which Sir Jealous Frantick adopts Spanish manners and virtually imprisons his daughter is based on *The Gentleman Dancing-Master*. Felix's jealousy of Violante in *The Wonder* (1714) recalls *Love in a Wood*, in which Valentine is also in hiding after a duel and suspects Cristina's fidelity.

Centlivre does not 'flesh out' her characters, regarding this as the actor's work. Her preface to *The Wonder* asserts: 'The Poet and the Player are like Soul and Body, indispensably necessary to one Another; the correct Author makes the Player shine, whilst the judicious Player makes the Poet's Fame immortal.' Melinda C. Finberg calls her 'a consummate actor's writer' because the plays allow lead actors to demonstrate their versatility.

Centlivre belongs to a tradition that goes back through Shadwell, Jonson and the Roman playwright, Terence, whom she mentions in her dedication to *The Busy Body*. Structure is the prime consideration in her plays. Although her characters have individual traits, they are derived from stereotypes. The plays are short by Restoration standards, and brisk. Richard Cumberland evokes their energy: 'They have bustle, they have business.'

Cumberland selected *The Busy Body*, *The Wonder* and *A Bold Stroke for a Wife* for the seventh volume of his *British Drama* (1817) as Centlivre's best plays. *The Busy Body*, with its parallel stories in which two couples outwit their elders, is a comedy of manners. Isabinda is guarded by her Spanish-minded father, Sir Jealous Frantick, while Miranda pretends to love her corrupt guardian, Sir Francis, who means to marry her. Miranda is typical of Centlivre's tough-minded heroines; she protects her inheritance while setting out 'in pursuit of the young fellow she likes'. Marplot is a convincingly childlike character. He is the little boy who is never allowed to join the gang.

The Wonder, set in Portugal, is a 'Spanish' comedy of intrigue comparable to Aphra Behn's *The Rover*. Colonel Britton wishes for a woman and Isabella falls on him after escaping from her home by leaping from an upstairs window. Her brother, Don Felix, became David Garrick's favourite role; he played Violante's young lover into his late fifties. Don Pedro is one of Centlivre's exceptionally repressive fathers and wants Violante to enter a nunnery so that he may keep her fortune.

A Bold Stroke for a Wife (1718) is Centlivre's most inventive farce. Mrs Lovely is protected by four guardians. Her dying father 'hated posterity ... and wished the world were to expire with himself'. He chose men with widely differing values and stipulated that his daughter could only marry if they all approved. The Colonel adopts five disguises to gain their signatures on a document of consent. He imitates the linguistic habits of a beau, a scholar, a merchant and a Quaker. Finally, in Prim's home, the lovers describe their desire for each other in the religious language of their Quaker hosts:

Prim: My soul rejoiceth, yea, it rejoiceth, I say, to find the spirit within thee; for lo, it moveth thee with natural agitation – yea, with natural agitation, I say again, and stirreth up the seeds of thy virgin inclination towards this good man – yea, it stirreth, as one may say, yea, verily, I say, it stirreth up thy inclination – yea, as one would stir a pudding.

Mrs Lovely: I see, I see – the spirit guiding of thy hand, good Obadiah Prim, and now behold thou art signing thy consent.– And now I see myself within thy arms, my friend and brother, yea, I am become bone of thy bone and flesh of thy flesh (*embraces him*) – hum –

Colonel (*aside*) : Admirably performed.– And I will take thee in all spiritual love for an helpmeet, yea, for the wife of my bosom.– And now, methinks, I feel a longing – yea, a longing I say, for the consummation of thy love, hum – yea, I do long exceedingly.

Centlivre parodies the Quakers' impromptu religious exhortations inspired by their 'inner light'. She depicts the perils of improvisation by constant use of 'fillers' like repeated phrases, the quasi-biblical 'yeas' and the hesitant 'hums'. Prim's anti-climactic comparison of spiritual exaltation with the stirring of a pudding comes from his need to say something, anything, rather than dry up.

Fidelis Morgan, in *The Female Wits: Women Playwrights of the Restoration* (1981), treats Centlivre's death as the 'close [of] a chapter: by that time, women writers had another medium open to them: the novel.' Southerne, Vanbrugh, Farquhar and Centlivre all anticipate the plenitude of the novel in different ways but Restoration drama is of unique value in itself. It is England's greatest theatre of desire and the questioning of identity. While masked, Marguerite in *The Princess of Cleves* is courted by her unfaithful lover. In *The Wives' Excuse*, a masked Mrs Friendall is propositioned by her husband. Alcmena in *Amphitryon* shares her bed with Jupiter disguised as her husband. Monimia in *The Orphan* believes that she is lying with her husband on her wedding night when he has been supplanted by his brother. Wycherley uses the idea of lovers stumbling through darkness in three of his four plays. These multiplying examples raise questions of sexual identity. Do we ever see the object of our desire plainly? Our enduring image of Restoration drama, should not be of overdressed aristocrats indulging in endless small talk. Instead, the key symbols should be the mask, the sword and the erotic promise of a lover waiting in a darkened room.

Select Bibliography

The Plays

Aphra Behn, *Five Plays* (Methuen, 1994).

J. Douglas Canfield (general ed.), *The Broadview Anthology of Restoration and Early Eighteenth-Century Drama*, concise edn. (Broadview, 2004).

Susanna Centlivre, *The Basset Table*, ed. Jane Milling (Broadview, 2009).

    A Bold Stroke for a Wife, ed. Nancy Copeland (Broadview, 2005).

    The Wonder, ed. John O'Brien (Broadview, 2004).

William Congreve, *The Way of the World and Other Plays*, ed. Eric Rump (Penguin, 2006).

John Dryden, *All for Love*, ed. N.J. Andrew (New Mermaids, 2011).

Marriage à la Mode, ed. David Crane (New Mermaids, 2010).

George Etherege, *The Plays of George Etherege*, ed. Michael Cordner (Cambridge University Press, 2008).

The Man of Mode, ed. John Bernard (New Mermaids, 2010).

George Farquhar, *The Beaux' Stratagem*, ed. Ann Blake (New Mermaids, 2006).

The Recruiting Officer, ed. Tiffany Stern (New Mermaids, 2011).

Melinda C. Finberg (ed.), *Eighteenth-Century Women Dramatists* (Oxford University Press, 2008).

Deborah Payne Fisk (ed.), *Four Restoration Libertine Plays* (Oxford University Press, 2009).

Trevor R. Griffiths, and Simon Trussler (eds.), *Restoration Comedy* (Nick Hern, 2005).

Ben Jonson, *Epicoene*, ed. R.V. Holdsworth (New Mermaids, 1979).

Scott McMillan (ed.), *Restoration and Eighteenth-Century Comedy* (Norton, 1997).

Thomas Shadwell, *The Virtuoso*, ed. Marjorie Hope Nicolson and David Stuart Rodes. (University of Nebraska Press, 1966).

Sir John Vanbrugh, *The Relapse and Other Plays*, ed. Brean Hammond (Oxford University Press, 2004).

David Womersley (ed.), *Restoration Drama: An Anthology* (Blackwell, 2000).

WilliamWycherley, *The Country Wife and Other Plays*, ed. Peter Dixon (Oxford University Press, 2008).

Criticism and Background Reading

Kate Aughterson, *Aphra Behn: The Comedies.* (Palgrave, 2003).

Gilli Bush-Bailey, *Treading the Bawds* (Manchester University Press, 2009).

Simon Callow, *Acting in Restoration Comedy* (Applause, 1991).

Deborah Payne Fisk (ed.), *The Cambridge Companion to English Restoration Theatre.* (Cambridge University Press, 2000).

Anthony Fowles, *John Dryden* (Greenwich Exchange, 2003).

Susan J. Owen, *A Companion to Restoration Drama* (Blackwell, 2008).

Gillian Perry, Joseph Roach and Shearer West, *The First Actresses: Nell Gwyn to Sarah Siddons* (National Portrait Gallery, 2011).

Max Stafford-Clark, *Letters to George.* 1989 (Nick Hern, 2008).

Janet Todd (ed.), *Aphra Behn*, New Casebook Series (Macmillan, 1999).

David M.Vieth (ed.), *The Complete Poems of John Wilmot, Earl of Rochester* (New Haven, 2002).

George Woodcock, *The English Sappho* (Black Rose Books, 1989; originally published as *The Incomparable Aphra*, 1948).

GREENWICH EXCHANGE BOOKS

STUDENT GUIDE LITERARY SERIES

The Greenwich Exchange Student Guide Literary Series is a collection of essays on major or contemporary serious writers in English and selected European languages. The series is for the student, the teacher and the 'common reader' and is an ideal resource for libraries. The *Times Educational Supplement* praised these books, saying, "The style of [this series] has a pressure of meaning behind it. Readers should learn from that ... If art is about selection, perception and taste, then this is it."

The series includes:
Antonin Artaud by Lee Jamieson (978-1-871551-98-3)
W.H. Auden by Stephen Wade (978-1-871551-36-5)
Jane Austen by Pat Levy (978-1-871551-89-1)
Honoré de Balzac by Wendy Mercer (978-1-871551-48-8)
Louis de Bernières by Rob Spence (978-1-906075-13-2)
William Blake by Peter Davies (978-1-871551-27-3)
The Brontës by Peter Davies (978-1-871551-24-2)
Robert Browning by John Lucas (978-1-871551-59-4)
Lord Byron by Andrew Keanie (978-1-871551-83-9)
Samuel Taylor Coleridge by Andrew Keanie (978-1-871551-64-8)
Joseph Conrad by Martin Seymour-Smith (978-1-871551-18-1)
William Cowper by Michael Thorn (978-1-871551-25-9)
Charles Dickens by Robert Giddings (987-1-871551-26-6)
Emily Dickinson by Marnie Pomeroy (978-1-871551-68-6)
John Donne by Sean Haldane (978-1-871551-23-5)
Elizabethan Love Poets by John Greening (978-1-906075-52-1)
Ford Madox Ford by Anthony Fowles (978-1-871551-63-1)
Sigmund Freud by Stephen Wilson (978-1-906075-30-9)
The Stagecraft of Brian Friel by David Grant (978-1-871551-74-7)
Robert Frost by Warren Hope (978-1-871551-70-9)
Patrick Hamilton by John Harding (978-1-871551-99-0)
Thomas Hardy by Sean Haldane (978-1-871551-33-4)
Seamus Heaney by Warren Hope (978-1-871551-37-2)
Joseph Heller by Anthony Fowles (978-1-871551-84-6)
George Herbert By Neil Curry and Natasha Curry (978-1-906075-40-8)
Gerard Manley Hopkins by Sean Sheehan (978-1-871551-77-8)
James Joyce by Michael Murphy (978-1-871551-73-0)
Philip Larkin by Warren Hope (978-1-871551-35-8)

Laughter in the Dark – The Plays of Joe Orton by Arthur Burke
  (978-1-871551-56-3)
George Orwell by Warren Hope (978-1-871551-42-6)
Sylvia Plath by Marnie Pomeroy (978-1-871551-88-4)
Poets of the First World War by John Greening (978-1-871551-79-2)
Alexander Pope by Neil Curry (978-1-906075-23-1)
Philip Roth by Paul McDonald (978-1-871551-72-3)
Shakespeare's *A Midsummer Night's Dream* by Matt Simpson
  (978-1-871551-90-7)
Shakespeare's *As You Like It* by Matt Simpson (978-1-906075-46-0)
Shakespeare's *Hamlet* by Peter Davies (978-1-906075-12-5)
Shakespeare's *Julius Caesar* by Matt Simpson (978-1-906075-37-8)
Shakespeare's *King Lear* by Peter Davies (978-1-871551-95-2)
Shakespeare's *Macbeth* by Matt Simpson (978-1-871551-69-3)
Shakespeare's *The Merchant of Venice* by Alan Ablewhite
  (978-1-871551-96-9)
Shakespeare's *Much Ado About Nothing* by Matt Simpson
  (978-1-906075-01-9)
Shakespeare's Non-Dramatic Poetry by Martin Seymour-Smith
  (978-1-871551-22-8)
Shakespeare's *Othello* by Matt Simpson (978-1-871551-71-6)
Shakespeare's *Romeo and Juliet* by Matt Simpson (978-1-906075-17-0)
Shakespeare's Second Tetralogy: *Richard II–Henry V*
  by John Lucas (978-1-871551-97-6)
Shakespeare's Sonnets by Martin Seymour-Smith (978-1-871551-38-9)
Shakespeare's *The Tempest* by Matt Simpson (978-1-871551-75-4)
Shakespeare's *Twelfth Night* by Matt Simpson (978-1-871551-86-0)
Shakespeare's *The Winter's Tale* by John Lucas (978-1-871551-80-8)
Percy Bysshe Shelley by Andrew Keanie (978-1-871551-59-0)
Tobias Smollett by Robert Giddings (978-1-871551-21-1)
Alfred, Lord Tennyson by Michael Thorn (978-1-871551-20-4)
Dylan Thomas by Peter Davies (978-1-871551-78-5)
William Wordsworth by Andrew Keanie (978-1-871551-57-0)
W.B. Yeats by John Greening (978-1-871551-34-1)

FOCUS ON SERIES

(ISBN prefix 978-1-906075 applies to all the following titles):

Other subjects covered by Greenwich Exchange books
Biography
Education
Philosophy